Good Neighbors

INTERCULTURAL PRESS

A Nicholas Brealey Publishing Company

BOSTON • LONDON

The InterAct Series

Good Neighbors

COMMUNICATING WITH THE MEXICANS

SECOND EDITION

JOHN C. CONDON

INTERCULTURAL PRESS, INC.

First published by Intercultural Press, a Nicholas Brealey Publishing company, in 1985. Revised in 1997. For more information, contact:

Intercultural Press, Inc.
A division of
Nicholas Brealey Publishing
100 City Hall Plaza, Suite 501
Boston, MA 02108 USA
Tel: (+) 617-523-3801
Fax: (+) 617-523-3708
www.interculturalpress.com

Nicholas Brealey Publishing
3-5 Spafield Street
Clerkenwell
London, EC1R 4QB, UK
Tel: (+) 44-207-239-0360
Fax: (+) 44-207-239-0370
www.nicholasbrealey.com

Copyright © 1985, 1997 by Intercultural Press Inc.

ISBN-13: 978-1-877864-53-7
ISBN-10: 1-877864-53-6

The illustration on the cover and throughout the book is from recent Mexican pottery and represents the symbol of the Republic of Mexico.

Printed in the United States of America

11 10 09 08 07   7 8 9 10 11

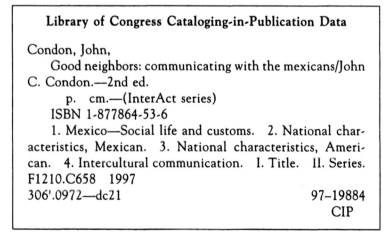

Library of Congress Cataloging-in-Publication Data

Condon, John,
    Good neighbors: communicating with the mexicans/John C. Condon.—2nd ed.
        p. cm.—(InterAct series)
    ISBN 1-877864-53-6
    1. Mexico—Social life and customs. 2. National characteristics, Mexican. 3. National characteristics, American. 4. Intercultural communication. I. Title. II. Series.
F1210.C658 1997
306'.0972—dc21   97-19884
                                      CIP

Contents

Foreword to the First Edition

If you are planning to do something with Mexicans, whether as a tourist, businessperson, student, teacher, or in any other role—either in the United States or in Mexico—you have chosen the right book to guide you.

As a Mexican and as a professional in the field of human communication, I have found this book to express very clearly what I have for a long time tried to tell my U.S. friends and students. It summarizes and exemplifies cultural differences and provides avenues to promote a successful dialogue.

Communication is an activity we have engaged in since we were born, and consequently we tend to take it for granted. If we know the language of a country, we tend to believe that we won't have problems communicating and that we will really get to know the people. Unfortunately, there is much more to communication than language alone.

This book is about communication. The reader will find considerations of language, norms, values, perception, nonverbal codes, and other issues which will enable him or her to adjust to and learn from the Mexican culture.

The people of Mexico and the United States have communicated for generations. However, this communication has been characterized by failures in many instances. This book has been needed for a long time and is finally published at the point in history when Mexico-U.S. relations must be improved for the sake of commerce, friendship, and perhaps, survival.

The typical U.S. traveler to Mexico may read a tourism guide, a manual, a history book, and perhaps an anthropological or sociological treatise. Not until now has the U.S. traveler had a practical book on communication. And communication is most of what we do when we interact with people. The way we look at people, the way we dress, the way we greet, the way we go about our business, all have different meanings to people who belong to different cultures.

Interestingly enough, this book is not just a collection of recipes, but a global and scholarly piece which, by being practical, satisfies the reader in search of tips to communicate more successfully, while at the same time providing the reader whose motives are more scholarly with a conceptual framework to understand and explain Mexican/U. S. communication.

This book may not only prove to be helpful to U.S. citizens but also to Mexicans interested in establishing a cultural dialogue with them. It provides a description of U.S. perceptions of Mexico and insights about the American character. After all, intercultural communication requires at least two individuals, and both need to be aware of the factors which affect their communication.

Eventually, through contributions like this book, physical nearness may be accompanied by psychological closeness as well.

—Felipe Korzenny
San Francisco State University

Preface to the Second Edition

It is with strong feelings and a great deal of pride that the Intercultural Press presents this revised and updated edition of *Good Neighbors*. It and its companion work *With Respect to the Japanese* were the first two volumes in the InterAct Series, and both were written by good friend and colleague Jack Condon. Not only did they inaugurate the series, they set the standard by which all subsequent titles have been measured.

Condon's experience in and his depth of understanding of the cultures he writes about, his economy and grace of style, and his ability to illuminate the practical issues in cross-cultural interaction while bringing scholarly perspectives to bear offer guiding principles not only for the InterAct Series but for any effective writing about intercultural subjects.

As a faculty member at the University of New Mexico, where he teaches intercultural communication, Condon has been able to maintain close contact with Mexican culture both inside Mexico and as it has developed in the border-lands of the southwestern United States. At the same time, he remains a perceptive observer of the culture of the United States as it has evolved in the late twentieth century. It is, of course, in that nexus between Mexican culture and that of its northern neighbor that a major dimension of U.S.-Mexican relations will be played out. Mexico is now the second largest trading partner of the United States and may soon be its largest. There are hundreds of thousands of U.S. citizens living and working in Mexico and millions of Mexicans and people of Mexican descent living in the United States. What this means is that the two countries, as Condon emphasizes, have not only had an immense influence on each other in the past but will continue to vitally affect one another into the future.

This revision of *Good Neighbors*, therefore, is timely and will continue to provide both practical guidance and food for thought to anyone with a need to understand the dynamics of the two cultures in contact.

Welcome to a rich reading experience.

—David S. Hoopes

Preface to the First Edition

North Americans need basic, practical guidelines on how to understand and communicate successfully with Mexicans. They must understand the process of cross-cultural interaction if they are to deal each day with the variety of new situations for which specific "do's and don'ts" may be misleading or are simply not available.

A *cultural interaction* study like this one probes, explains, and predicts what happens when individuals who have grown up in contrasting cultures meet, eat, joke, argue, negotiate, and cooperate with one another. Such a study makes clear what each person must do in order to become a clever competitor or a trusted colleague and friend.

This volume, therefore, and the other volumes in the InterAct Series, explain how people from one culture see those in another; what exactly they expect from each other; how they affect each other when they are together; and how what is said and done by one embarrasses, frustrates, motivates, impresses, or angers the other.

We have chosen to analyze Mexican-North American relations in this volume because of Mexico's special importance to the United States and because North Americans often seriously misunderstand Mexicans. We were fortunate that John Condon was available to prepare the study.

John is not only one of the most insightful intercultural specialists in the field, he is keenly aware of the difficulties and opportunities experienced by Americans and Mexicans in their social and business relationships. Some of his most effective work has been with international business firms preparing American personnel and their families for assignments in other countries, and with overseas personnel assuming responsibilities in the United States. Fortunately, John is also an outstanding writer, having completed a dozen books on communication including one, *An Introduction to Intercultural Communication*, which has for many years been a standard textbook in the field.

John's experience in Mexico began in 1956 when he entered the University of the Americas. He returned there a few years later to conduct his doctoral research, then again in 1974 to teach and do further studies. In 1987-1988 he taught at the University of Guadalajara, and he has returned frequently since.

Felipe Korzenny agreed enthusiastically when we invited him to write the Foreword for the book. Felipe is a citizen of Mexico and a professor at San Francisco State University, where he teaches graduate and undergraduate courses in intercultural communication. He serves frequently as a consultant to the government of Mexico and as a consultant to the U. S. Agency for International Development in Mexico and in a number of other Latin American countries. In these countries, and among Hispanic Americans in the United States, Felipe has conducted communication studies in several areas, including an area in which he has special interest and expertise: the effect of mass media upon social change.

We are confident that the readers of this book, if they consider carefully the explanations and follow the suggestions, will enjoy more thoroughly their association with Mexicans and will be able to work more productively with them.

—George W. Renwick
Editor, InterAct Series

Introduction

"Poor Mexico," lamented that nation's last prerevolutionary president, Porfirio Díaz, "so far from God, so near the United States." While Mexico's current proximity to the Lord may be a subject of some debate, no one can dispute that in nearly every way Mexico has never been closer to its neighbor to the north. The fifteen-hundred-mile border that spans the continent is crossed in both directions by more people than any other international boundary in the world. The traffic heading south annually includes millions of tourists. Tourism is a major source of income for Mexico, and 80 percent of the tourists come from the United States. And northward come the Mexicans: over one million five hundred thousand a year enter the United States with visas while another 96,000, it is estimated, cross in the shadows, without papers or legal protection.

Mexico's capital city is now the world's most populous, with all the richness and problems such a distinction suggests. By the end of this decade it is estimated that Mexico City will be the home of 32 million people, a number particularly sobering to this writer who knew the city in the 1950s when the population of all of Mexico was only 32 million.

Moreover, along the coastal cities on the Pacific, from Alaska to Argentina, Los Angeles is the second largest city, followed by (can you guess): Tijuana! The maquiladoras, especially, have lured millions of Mexicans to Tijuana and other border cities.

Since the signing of the North American Free Trade Agreement (NAFTA) in 1992, Mexico is a partner in a "free trade zone" that may comprise the largest market in the world. To this expanding market Mexico brings nearly 90 million people. NAFTA and manufacturing and marketing choices, in turn, involve countless numbers of other North Americans in daily communication with Mexicans. The economic, political, and social impact of these new relationships is felt on both sides of the border, with no lack of critics or supporters in Mexico as well as in the United States. The fact is that even without a formal arrangement between governments, the social and economic ties between Mexico and the United States have never been so extensive. Already Mexico is the third largest trading partner of the United States.

The "cultural exports"—including music, TV shows, foods—are clearly more prominent today than ever before. In the United States there are increasing numbers of Spanish-language TV outlets; cable TV transmits U.S. programs to those with the money and the desire to watch them in Mexico. Fast-food chains featuring tacos or burritos now dot the U.S. landscape, just as the hamburger, pancake, and fried chicken dispensaries have emerged in Mexico.

Mexican foods now seem as American as pizza pie. Corn chips for snacking now outsell potato chips in the United States, and salsa outsells ketchup as a condiment.

As so often occurs in international lending and borrowing of foods—and words—what is believed to have come from one side of the border was in fact created on the other side. "Nachos," for example, is a U.S. concoction—as are fajitas and chimichangas. And to complete the process, all are now served up in Mexico, with many Mexicans and North Americans convinced that they originated in Mexico.

Icons of pop culture from the United States are everywhere

in Mexico, even in traditional Mexican genres such as pina-
tas and ceramic miniatures.

In urban Mexico, especially, traditional Mexican holiday
celebrations show the influence from the north, as Santa
Claus has edged out the traditional Three Kings who would
bring gifts for children on January sixth, Epiphany Day, and
U.S. Halloween motifs haunt the traditional features of *el Día
de los Muertos*, the Day of the Dead.

Video rental stores are stocked with more films from the
United States than from Mexico, though Enrique Sanchez of
the University of Guadalajara reports, with some irony, that
the largest number of Mexican movie rentals are to be found
in Mexico's Blockbuster Video outlets.

But for all the burgeoning presence of things Mexican in
the United States, there is still an imbalance. Studies show
that the average Mexico City daily newspaper contains a
higher percentage of news about the United States than the
average issue of the *New York Times* contains about all the
rest of the world combined.

More important is the evidence that despite the intertwin-
ing of population, culture, and destiny, there is still a great
gap in understanding. For many persons in the United States,
the image of the Mexican has been that of the *bracero*, the
migrant farm laborer, or a cartoon caricature, Chiquita Banana or Frito Bandito. The old negative images are still
perceptible, as in advertising slogans like Taco Bell's "Make
a run for the border." (That fast-food chain itself has, like
many other North American franchises, now entered the
Mexican market.) U.S. products, including media products,
accelerated their numbers and their appeal among Mexicans,
especially younger Mexicans. The trade agreement will no
doubt only increase this further. And there remains the distrust by many Mexicans of *yanqui* power, economic and political, even as the presence of the United States in Mexico
parallels the Mexican impact on the United States. Though
the number is increasing, relatively few North Americans

have had much direct contact with the Mexican executive, doctor, professor, or engineer. For many Mexicans, the stereotypic American straddles the Rio Grande with a greedy eye and bags of money in each hand. Some observers believe that the kinds of superficial contacts Mexicans and North Americans have actually increase rather than decrease the likelihood of serious culture-based breakdowns in their relations.

During his highly successful visit to Mexico in 1962, John Kennedy proclaimed that "Geography has made us neighbors, tradition has made us friends." It was a welcome and optimistic thought, but this writer's research at the time showed that most Mexicans felt it more accurate to say "Geography has made us closer, tradition has made us far apart."

Now, over three decades later, we seem no closer. Friendship is a fragile bloom, nurtured more by need than knowledge. Too little has been done to encourage Americans and Mexicans to come to grips with the fact that in a number of critical ways their views of the world differ radically and that these differences raise important barriers to effective communication and mutually satisfactory working relationships. They each assume that what they know about the other is enough. But it isn't. More is needed. This book is designed for those who recognize that need and are willing to put their minds to it. Such an effort will be triply rewarded: in being better able to appreciate the realities encountered in Mexico and dealing with them more effectively; in avoiding some of the foolish mistakes which arise out of cultural naivete; and in being able to convey an attitude of respect and concern which can often make the difference between success and failure in communicating across cultures.

—John Condon
Albuquerque, 1997

1

The Role of History

It is ironic that many people in the United States think of
Mexico as the "land of *mañana*" when, as any advertising
copywriter will tell you, it is north of the border that "tomor-
row" is the magic word. Our mental compasses point to a
future just over the horizon from which all our other directions are set.

As much as the future pulls us forward, the past propels
Mexican thought and action. Not that the future in Mexico
is ignored, far from it. Everything in Mexico, problems to be
dealt with and potentials to be realized, calls for planning
based on projections: the swelling of the population, the
debilitating effects of air pollution, the growing economic
and political role in the hemisphere, and more—these are
part of a mañana discussed in every newpaper and magazine
in the country. But at least as frequent are the essays and
editorials which look back into history for direction and
guidance.

A North American executive, with nearly twenty-five years
of experience in and out of Mexico, put it this way:

> Like many Americans of my day, I came to Mexico impressed
> with its modern art, its futuristic architecture, and its prom-
> ise. I always saw Mexico as the land of the future, and history

1

didn't really interest me. Frankly, I thought that history books were for tourists who were afraid to go out and see the real Mexico. Later I came to see that I was the romantic tourist. To really understand Mexico and the United States, I realized I had to look more carefully at the past. When I give advice to Americans coming down here to do business, I tell them: study history. Start with it and continue with it. Apart from the language itself, I don't know of anything that will prepare you better and make you more "respectable" in the eyes of your [Mexican] co-workers. If anybody had told me that twenty-five years ago, I would have smiled and gone on reading the *Wall Street Journal*. Which, in fact, is just what most Mexicans expect us to do.

Indeed, a comparison of histories goes a long way in explaining the differences in outlook and behavior of people on both sides of the border. We usually trace our history from a specific date—1607 with the founding of Jamestown or 1620 and the Pilgrims and Plymouth. We think of the United States as a kind of enterprise with "founding fathers" and certain principles the organization was designed to follow. We also see our history as moving in a straight line from a particular date in history. The dates which as children we learn at school are nearly all dates of battles won, territory added to the union, or some other positive achievement. As if in a speeded-up film, we visualize our country expanding westward; time and space are conjoined in a steady progression. The West was won, we say; we give little thought to anything being lost. It sounds just right, American in itself, to speak of "the making of America." The "taking" of America is not part of our lore.

The people already living on the continent when the English arrived were hunters, herders, fishermen. They had erected no great cities or monuments to rival anything in Europe, and their cultures held little interest for the colonists so long as they could be displaced and their land cultivated. The North American Indian has remained excluded from the shaping of the dominant culture of the new nation just as he had been excluded from the land. As the nation took shape, the outlook was to the future, to new and mostly hospitable land, to new opportunities. A spirit of optimism animated this movement.

The land that became the United States was, for the most part, rich, and for much of the nation's short history, seemingly endless. Thus anyone, the national myth had it, could make his or her way in this world. There was opportunity for all: was not this why so many left their homelands to settle here? A land of promise, it was, that only asked that one work hard or move westward to push back the frontier.

The Mexican story was different. The land had been populated for centuries by warring tribes numbering in the hundreds (even today about 150 different languages are still spoken in Mexico); there was no frontier. In most tribes, certainly in the dominant tribes such as the earlier Mayans and the late-flourishing Aztecs, class lines were rigid as though etched in stone, justified and maintained in a theocratic state.

The land itself was not accommodating. Volcanoes above, tremors below, only a small portion level. Even today no more than a fifth of the land is arable. Here was a land that nurtured fatalism. It remains today for millions of *campesinos* a realistic expectation that the future will be no better save for the grace of one's *patron* or, in today's cities, through a stroke of luck as in winning the lottery.

Centuries before Cortez arrived in Mexico, civilizations unrivaled by anything known in Europe at that time had flourished, declined, disappeared. What happened to some remains a mystery today, even though the Mexican government spends more of its budget on anthropological research to uncover the past than does any other country. Why, for instance, did the sophisticated Mayan empire come to an abrupt end? Was it because of disease, war, revolution? It happened centuries before America was "discovered."

The society that Cortez encountered in 1519 was a relatively new power which in a short time had subdued rival tribes and imposed a fierce theocratic state. The Aztec society was caste-based, with political power shared by the religious and military chiefs. In some respects it mirrored the ethos of Spain in the first half of the sixteenth century.

In less than two years, Cortez and his soldiers had completed the conquest, eventually extending Spanish dominion south into Central America and as far north as Alaska. What we in the United States generally refer to as "the Southwest" is accurately named in terms of U.S. geography. But in terms of its historic and cultural ties for over five hundred years, "the Southwest" might better be called "the Northwest." Spain ruled Mexico for the next three centuries. How it was that a small band of European soldiers were able to become the *conquistadores* of such a vast and powerful empire in so short a time cannot be answered in these pages, but there are those who find in its answer contemporary meanings. Some say it was largely due to a kind of fatalism one can discern in Mexico today, in songs, in jokes, in celebrations such as the Day of the Dead. Some say that it had to do with a conception of time as cyclical which, while not uniquely Mexican, is quite different from the progressive line of time as conceived in the United States. All agree that for the Aztecs then, as for many Mexicans today, the natural and the supernatural were not separate. In Mexico, all events are "acts of God," not just those which in the United States are so chancy that insurance companies exclude them from coverage.

The Spanish who came to Mexico were from all parts of Spain and all classes, backgrounds, regions, and religions. Sephardic Jews from southern Spain, fleeing the forced conversions and impending Inquisition, were a substantial part of the early Spanish presence in Mexico. It has been estimated that by 1545 a fourth of the Spaniards in Mexico City were Jews and that by the 1600s perhaps half of the European population of Mexico City was Jewish.

There was also an African presence, with estimates of as many as three hundred black Moors accompanying Cortez on his conquest. It had been a scant twenty-five years since the Spanish had driven from Spain the last of the Moorish leaders whose Arabic influence was stamped on so much that we think of as Spanish: the ceramic tiles, the arches, the wrought-iron work, and even attitudes about the proper relations between men and women. Many in the United States are surprised to discover so many similarities between Mexico and the Arabic-speaking world of the Middle East.

Little wonder, then, that there is in Mexico today, and has been for many years, a serious pursuit of the question "Who is the Mexican?" The search for answers has led in many directions, particularly back to the traumatic birth nearly five hundred years ago which produced *la raza*, "the cosmic race," and a glorification of Latin culture. As that research continues we should not lose sight of the role the North American plays in the Mexican's attempts to understand himself.

In the years ahead we may also find that Mexicans will be joined by many others, including their neighbors to the north, seeking the answer to the question "Who is the Mexican?" Americans are only now discovering the vast and deep culture that is Mexico.

2

Taking Stock of One Another

The images which Americans and Mexicans have of themselves and of each other, historically, began to take shape not so much in the Spanish and English colonies of the "New World" as in England and Europe. Spain and England were, of course, rivals. And if they had common goals of controlling the seas and expanding their empires, they differed in language, religion, and other primary features of culture. Mutual distrust and anti-Hispanic sentiment among the English, which began even before the age of the New World conquest, slowly evolved into the *leyenda negra*, the black legend.

Leyenda Negra

The myth of the leyenda negra illustrated for most North Americans the superiority of their colonization to that of the Spaniards. The English settlers, we learn as children in the United States, were not afraid of hard physical work, while the Spaniard, whether soldier or aristocrat, disdained manual labor.

This distinction, between the humble and hardworking English settler who escaped English rule and the royalist Spanish soldier and aristocrat who conquered and imposed

7

Catholicism on the indigenous peoples of the Americas, became central to the black legend. The religious differences between Protestantism and Catholicism were emphasized, and a backwash of hatred and rumors about Spanish cruelty, the Inquisition, the lust for gold, and other "facts" and opinions were repeated from generation to generation in stories and in books. The impact of the leyenda negra became as strong in Europe as it was in what the Europeans called the New World.

In Latin America, even among those who have been highly critical of the Spanish conquest, an opposing myth has evolved which says that the Latin American raza, or "race" (culturally defined), is superior to that which exists in North America. La Raza is superior, moreover, because of the very elements which were most brutally condemned in the leyenda negra, namely what the Spanish contributed to the Indians of the New World out of which came the mestizo. Not the Inquisition but the living faith of the Catholic missionaries, and the humanistic and spiritual life which they fostered, are praised and contrasted with the history of the Anglo-Saxon colonists. Mexican Nobel Prize-winning author Octavio Paz says:

> The Church used the key of baptism to open the doors of society, converting it into a universal order open to everyone.... This possibility of belonging to a living order, even if it was at the bottom of the social pyramid, was cruelly denied to the Indians by the Protestants of New England. It is often forgotten that to belong to the Catholic faith meant that one found a place in the cosmos. The flight of their gods and the death of their leaders had left the natives in a solitude so complete that it is difficult for a modern man to imagine it. Catholicism re-established their ties with the world and the other world.[1]

In the secular expressions of the spirit, too, Latin Americans feel they excel their Saxon neighbors to the north. Art, literature, and music are contrasted with trade, money, and machines, which the North Americans are believed to value. These contrasts are expressed in many forms, including in the symbolism of Diego Rivera and other Mexican muralists, and in many Chicano murals in this country.

Many Mexicans grow up in a culture of ambivalent feelings about the United States, involving both distrust and attraction. A Mexican may confide, for example, that while he or she would prefer to buy something *hecho en Mexico*, there is also the belief that something made in the United States will be superior.

If the black legend has diminished somewhat over the centuries, its echoes can still be clearly heard when economic stresses and political conflicts arise in the United States. One can hear it in the rhetoric of some of the most strident critics of NAFTA, including in the televised remarks of H. Ross Perot, or when "illegal immigration" or drugs become useful domestic political prejudices to exploit. Many of the themes and the prejudices they draw upon date back five hundred years. What may be new, however, is that the rhetoric of public figures in the United States, as well as official programs such as building a wall along the border, are now broadcast on television throughout Mexico, too. Too often this confirms Mexican suspicions about attitudes and motives of those "good neighbors" to the north.

A particularly unattractive image of North Americans was described two generations ago in a study of images held by Mexican students prior to attending college in the States. This image has not disappeared over the years.

> Before arrival, [the Mexicans] believed the United States to be rich and highly mechanized; to have a high standard of living, large cities, big buildings, and a rush of traffic. Perhaps even more than do most Latin Americans or Asians, the Mexican student considered the United States to have a materialistic society with little regard for humanistic values,

for music, art, literature, or indeed any sense of the true meaning of life. Predominantly, although a student might know of exceptions, he believed that a citizen of the United States was concerned with gaining money and material goods. As a crass people they were believed lacking in manners, to have no family life, their children to be undisciplined, and divorce to be commonplace. American men do not love their wives, the Mexicans felt, because they let them do as they please. The freedom of women and girls was thought to mean sexual immorality. To the Mexican Catholic, the United States is a Protestant country peopled by followers of religious ideas he has been taught to abhor. But even these they do not really put into practice, and hence the United States is believed to be an irreligious country.[2]

The investigators believed that these opinions, unflattering as they are, were more positive than those held by the average Mexican. Following their studies in the United States, the Mexican students seem to break down many of their rigid stereotypes; nevertheless:

The Mexican student remained convinced, almost without exception, of the superiority of the Mexican life goals with their emphasis on spiritual and humanistic values. He further remained or even became a more confirmed Mexican nationalist.[3]

Mexicans will tell you that the past is past—*el arroz ya se cocinó*, the rice is cooked. But Mexicans know that U.S. troops in the nineteenth century marched all the way to the center of Mexico City and extracted as tribute territory that included Texas, New Mexico, Arizona, and California. There is a prominent monument at the entry to Chapultepec Park where the boy heroes, *los niños héroes*, were said to have wrapped themselves in the Mexican flag and jumped to their death rather than surrender. We sing about that site in the opening words of the Marine Hymn, though few may give much thought to those "Halls of Montezuma."[4] Troops stormed across the border again in the twentieth century, led by General Pershing hot in pursuit of Pancho Villa. Many Mexicans believe that their "good neighbor" to the north is not reluctant to throw its weight around when it wants something. There is the perception that more arrogant than ususal self-interest is the primary motivation in good relations with Mexico, whether it was fear of Fidel Castro more than thirty years ago or eagerness for free trade more recently.

While one may argue that all this has more to do with politics than business, to Mexicans these seem much more closely related than they might to some North Americans. A very important part of the revolutionary movement which overthrew the dictator Díaz and launched the modern Mexican state was anti-foreignism. Particularly strong feelings were directed against North American businessmen, who were the most visible of the wealthy and influential entrepreneurs. We in the United States have no experience in our history which is in any way comparable.

Vision of a Cosmic Race

The spiritual unity of all of Latin America is la raza. It is not the mestizo, per se, who is exalted in the myth of la raza, but often a mystical idealization of Latin culture.

Since the Revolution in 1910, the theme of la raza has aided in the unification of Mexico by celebrating the Indians and bringing them into the mainstream of the culture, though in recent times there has been a marked worsening in the attitude of the government and the general public toward the Indians. The motto of the National Autonomous University of Mexico (UNAM) is *"Por mi raza hablará el espíritu"* (Through my race the spirit will speak). This vision is not uniquely Mexican. Some see it as an intense continuation of the ideas of Simón Bolívar and other pan-American heroes who saw Spanish America as a single entity. Said one contemporary Mexican philosopher, "The American will become, with centuries, the sum and synthesis of humanity, spiritually as well as physically."

Psychological Profile of the Mexican

Important as the idea of a cosmic race may be in understanding a vision held by many Mexicans, it is just as important to look at another image: fragmentation and despair. In nearly every book or article on the subject of the Mexican's search for identity—and there is no shortage of such explorations—one encounters the theme of a brooding child, of the violent union of the Spanish father who abandoned his offspring and returned to Europe with the violated and still suffering Indian mother. Few contemporary interpreters of Mexican behavior fail to relate their views to those of Samuel Ramos in his book *Profile of Man and Culture*,[5] written in the 1940s and influenced by Alfred Adler's psychological theories of the time. Ramos propounded the idea of a "national inferiority complex" as a feature of Mexican "national character."

In his influential work, Ramos saw the Mexican as a child before an authoritarian parent. Ramos compares preconquest Mexico with Egypt, saying that for each culture, time produced little or no change. The sudden rupture of this tranquility, fierce as it was, toppling both gods and ancestors, produced a demoralization which is characteristic of the individual Mexican today. Though there is some dispute about the immutability of the preconquest period, the fact is that the conquest completely destroyed the traditional society and its beliefs. Moreover, forced to imitate the ways of the new master, not understanding them fully, the Mexican remained childlike. Ramos saw the process of imitation, first of Spain, then of France, and later of the United States, as a defense for the Mexican against feelings of inferiority.

In art, too, Ramos saw little originality as a result of the history of Mexico. The Mexican today, Ramos argued, is not an artist but an artisan who manufactures his works using an ability learned by tradition. The Revolution to some extent freed the artists as it freed all Mexicans from adherence to imitation and mental or political subjugation to foreign ideas, but popular contemporary Mexican artists still complain of a "cactus curtain" in art. The *sarapes*, pottery, and miscellaneous artifacts that delight the tourist are in conception thousands of years old.

In his home too, the Ramos thesis runs, the Mexican is a child before an authoritarian parent. Like the Spanish forefather, the immediate father makes demands on his children for obedience and love, with little display of these in return. And like the Spaniard before him, the father may abandon his children when he chooses. If he does not abandon them fully, he rarely appears among them, and even at these times, Ramos commented, he may return home drunken or angry. This harsh depiction by Ramos is echoed in many more contemporary Mexican movies, television dramas, and *fotonovelas* (photo stories), in which the most emotionally moving relationship is usually between the long-suffering mother and her sons.

The qualities that Ramos identified are exemplified in the Mexican *pelado*. A pelado is, literally, "the plucked one," the one at the bottom of the social pecking order who, having nobody elso to lord it over, exerts his authority over his wife and children. Perhaps the most popular characterization of one variety of pelado was that so often portayed by Cantinflas, Mexico's beloved and world-renowned comedian. Cantinflas (a name suggesting a bar [*cantina*] fly) was brilliant in using subterfuge and double-talk to make his way through a difficult world. He was the pelado who was the marginal character, more attractive in his picaresque existence than through his verbal aggressiveness, which abounds in sexual innuendos.

Mexican psychologist Francisco Gonzalez Pineda, who has written much on the Mexican character, also sees in the pelado the purist form of this Mexican type and values him for his rejection of middle-class morality. But according to Ramos, the pelado's quarrels and sexual exploits are not the result of any general animosity toward humanity but rather are sought by him to satisfy his own ego. In a world in which he is otherwise impotent, virility is his salvation. (See chapter 5 on Sex Roles and Sexuality.)

Is it paradoxical that a vision of a cosmic race should appear in a culture described as suffering from a national inferiority complex? Not at all. Idealism is one reaction to a history of defeat and frustration. Díaz-Guerrero offers a psychological interpretation of "the IFD syndrome": idealization—exaggerated fantasies of wealth, power, or machismo—leads inevitably to frustration which in turn leads to demoralization.

By whatever interpretation, the mixture of high ideals and sometime bravura helps to give the Mexican a quality that is different from other Latin Americans. Like the mixtures one finds in Mexican cooking—a *mole* of chiles and chocolate, for example—the blend of *picante* and *dulce* is surprising and delightful.

Living with Death

It is often said that one cannot understand Mexican life without comprehending the Mexican's view of death. In a famous essay, Octavio Paz contrasts attitudes north and south of the border:

> The word death is not pronounced in New York...because it burns the lips. The Mexican, in contrast, is familiar with death, jokes about it, caresses it, sleeps with it, celebrates it; it is one of his favorite toys and his most steadfast love.[6]

Compare two holidays which share a common religious past and coincide on the calendar, Halloween in the United States and the Day of the Dead in Mexico. In the United

States there are ghosts and skeletons that appear that day, but they are mostly symbolic, like the colors orange and black which identify the day as Halloween. Or they appear in costumes worn by children who go door-to-door in pursuit of what the day really means to them, a chance to accumulate treasures of candy.

In Mexico, the Día de los Muertos is a time to commune with the dead. Special breads are prepared, candy skulls and coffins are confected, many personalized with the names of those who would partake of them. Songs are sung and broadsides are distributed in the streets in which death dances with the rich and powerful, the pope and president no less than the ordinary person. Meals are set for the dead at many homes, and the cemeteries take on a festive air.

Equally surprising to many North American visitors are the images of Christ in Mexican churches, so real and detailed are the expressions of agony; these are no mere symbols. The visitor may also be surprised to see in one of those wonderfully elaborate crèche scenes at Christmas the presence of a devil or two, just as images of grinning skeletons appear in virtually all forms of folk art. Mexican newspaper accounts of traffic accidents shock the outsider unprepared for their vivid details. And there is the bullfight. As another Mexican writer says:

> To the Mexican...death is a bosom friend. Our people live with death; they seat it, literally, at their table and they invite it to share their bed. Beginning with childhood, the Mexican encounters death in a thousand different forms, images, and shapes.... One plays with death, one makes it the butt of jokes, prompted by a spirit of camaraderie, as if the exotic personage were an old and well-known friend of the Mexican.[7]

[1] Octavio Paz. *The Labyrinth of Solitude: Life and Thought in Mexico*. (New York: Grove Press, 1961), 26.

[2] Ralph L. Beals and Norman D. Humphrey. *No Frontier to Learning: The Mexican Student in the United States*. (Minneapolis: University of Minnesota Press, 1957), 50.

[3] Ibid., 50.

[4] Actually the name is "Moctezuma," with a *c* and not an *n*. The Spaniards, not the U.S. Marines, are to blame for the error, but the sensitive visitor will want to pronounce the name of the Aztec leader correctly.

[5] Samuel Ramos, *Profile of Man and Culture*. Austin, TX: University of Texas Press, 1962.

[6] Paz, *Labyrinth of Solitude*, 57.

[7] Emilio Uranga. "The Mexican Idea of Death," *Texas Quarterly* (Spring 1959), 53-54.

3

Varieties of
Individualism, North and South

The history of relations between the United States and Mexico has not been one of understanding and cooperation, though there is reason to hope that things will continue to improve as persons on both sides of the border work toward those ends. The role of the private citizen in day-to-day business and professional activities is crucial. Mexicans and North Americans working together sometimes feel confused, irritated, distrustful, even under the best of conditions and with the best of intentions. The causes lie not in the short-comings of either culture but rather in their interaction. Differences in values and styles of behavior are what Americans must look at in order to explain the conflicts and find ways to establish effective and productive working relationships.

The importance of the individual appears at first to be a fundamental value shared by Americans and Mexicans. Were persons from each culture to proceed on such an assumption, however, their talk would soon deteriorate into argument, with persons on each side convinced that their culture is the one that truly values the individual while the other's society patently does not. Eventually it becomes apparent that what

North Americans mean and what Mexicans mean when talking about the importance of the individual are not the same at all.

Individualism, American Style

In the North American value system are three central and interrelated assumptions about human beings. These are (1) that people, apart from social and educational influences, are basically the same; (2) that each person should be judged on his or her own individual merits; and (3) that these merits, including a person's worth and character, are revealed through the person's actions. Values of equality and independence—constitutional rights, laws, and social programs—arise from these assumptions. Because a person's actions are regarded as so important, it is the comparison of accomplishments—Mr. Johnson compared to Mr. Johnson's father, or Johnson five years ago compared to Johnson today, or Johnson compared to Jones and Smith—that provides a chief means of judging or even knowing a person.

The Mexican's "Inner Spirit"

In Mexico it is the uniqueness of the individual which is valued, a quality which is assumed to reside within each person and which is not necessarily evident through actions or achievements. It is closer to our notion of "soul" than "character." That inner quality which represents the dignity of each person must be protected at all costs; any action or remark that may be interpreted as a slight to the person's dignity is to be regarded as a grave provocation. Moreover, since a Mexican will most often regard him- or herself first of all as part of a family and only secondarily as a member of his or her profession, trade, or organization, a slight to any other family member will be as provocative as a direct insult.

This contrast, which is sometimes expressed as the distinction between "individualism" in the case of the North American and "individuality" in the case of the Mexican, frequently leads to misunderstandings in intercultural encounters, from small talk to philosophical arguments.

Where a Mexican will refer to a person's inner qualities in terms of the person's soul or spirit (*alma* or *espíritu*), North Americans are likely to feel uncomfortable using such words in reference to people. We tend to regard that kind of talk as vague or sentimental, the words seeming to describe something invisible and hence unknowable, or at the very least "too personal." For many North Americans such talk may be acceptable in some religious context, but that too is usually regarded as a private matter. Very little in our experience has prepared us to express those kinds of feelings openly; we may express our discomfort instead or attempt to change the subject to something more to our liking. This unwillingness to talk about the inner qualities of an individual can communicate to Mexicans that North Americans are, as suspected, insensitive and not really interested in the individual.

Equality as a value (if not always as a practice) requires of North Americans a good deal of positive conformity to social rules or principles. We believe it is both wise and normal to try to obey the law and to practice fair play. "Fair play" is said to be among the most difficult expressions to translate fully into other languages because of all it evokes from its English history. This is satirized in the old joke about two English sportsmen who, with their hounds, are in the woods hunting: one sees some movement in the brush and fires, whereupon the other exclaims "Good lord, man, you nearly shot my dog!" To which the first responds, "Terribly sorry; here, have a shot at mine." So far as I know this is a U.S. joke that plays on a stereotype of the Englishman who overdoes this "fairness business," but which is also funny because the American recognizes something of his or her own culture here. Americans are similarly made the butt of jokes by Mexicans and other Latinos for their seemingly excessive attention to abstract principles, which detracts from more immediate or personal matters.

We trust rules and we would like to trust others to obey those rules so that everybody has the same opportunities and obligations. A Mexican friend once remarked that he was shocked when he discovered that in the United States a driver would stop at a red light late at night when there was no other traffic around. "I used to think you had surrendered to your machines. Now I see that you are actually governed by certain abstract principles." He added that, in his opinion, "No Mexican would ever stop like that—not a real Mexican!"

In the United States, the ideal of being fair is supposed to transcend the desire to be loyal or to win at any cost. Any objective account of U.S. history would indicate that such has not been our practice, and in any case we offer our own inconsistent *dichos* (sayings). Compare "It's not whether you win or lose, it's how you play the game" with Vince Lombardi's "Winning isn't everything, it's the only thing."

Many Mexicans will pick up the mixed messages—that sometimes there is a fairness, often codified in laws, which exceeds comparable behavior in Mexico, but sometimes prejudice or simple selfishness contradicts the ideals.

As we shall see elsewhere, Mexicans, far more often than their North American counterparts, may ignore some abstract principle in favor of a very real person. Thus it is that a Mexican taxi driver may stop to pick up a friend he sees walking along the street, even while he has a paying passenger in the backseat, or bus drivers may engage in an impromptu race down the boulevard, even as their passengers are shouting that they want to be let off at their stop.

Tensions may arise between Mexicans and North Americans over what seems to be a conflict between trusting particular individuals or trusting abstract principles. In a business enterprise, the North American manager is likely to view the organization and its processes as primary, with the role of specific people being more or less supportive of that system. People can be replaced if need be; nobody is indispensable. When one places emphasis on a person's spirit or views an organization as if it were a family, however, then it seems just as clear that nobody can be exactly replaced by another. This is not to say that a Mexican organization is one big happy family. There are jealousies, rivalries, and petty— sometimes nasty—competitions that a North American manager soon becomes aware of. But the feeling of being a part of the company, the meaning of the relationship with others and the expectations about how one should be treated are different from those of a comparable organization north of the border.

One situation in which the difference is sometimes apparent is when two people compete for a promotion. An American manager with experience in both countries put it this way:

> In Mexico, Ricardo and Robert may compete in more personal terms but usually not openly. They are less likely to think of themselves as competing in their ability to help the organization than simply in their ability as such, because each considers himself the better person. Some see this dramatization of personal ability, including power, influence, and pride, as the Mexican male showing his machismo; others would describe it as a demonstration of leadership. [See also chapter 5.] It is really both because the two overlap so. In a boxing match the referee says, "May the best man win." To North Americans, that means that it will be fair if the person who is better at boxing wins the match. In Mexico, I think, people really want the *best man* to win.

Respect and Respeto

Both North Americans and Mexicans may speak of the need to respect another person, but here too the meaning of the word "respect" (or *respeto*) differs somewhat across cultures.

In a study of associations with this word conducted in both countries, it was found that Americans regarded respect as bound up with the values of equality, fair play, and democratic spirit. There were no emotional overtones. One respects others as one might respect the law.

For Mexicans, however, respect was much more emotionally charged, involving matters of power, possible threat, and often a love-hate relationship. The meaning of respect in Mexico arises from powerful human relationships, such as between a father and son, or patron and peon. In such cases it is as if fate or circumstances outside of one's control determined the relationship in the first place, and both parties recognize that they are unequal in their power and influence. There may be feelings of guilt that too much was asked for or too little given, or resentment that not enough was given or that very little was asked and even that reluctantly given. In any case, in Mexico the matter of respect is likely to be more personal and more a matter of circumstance, while for Americans respect is more a matter of principles to which individuals voluntarily commit themselves.

A Mexican manager may command respect by virtue of his position, age, or influence; the North American manager more likely wishes to earn respect through achievements or particular fair-minded relationships with his or her subordinates. Thus it is that American managers in Mexico often try to prove something that their Mexican employees have already assumed, while at the same time assuming much that their employees have yet to see demonstrated. A Mexican sales manager of a U.S. firm recalled one American vice president who, he says, "tried to 'win' our respect by showing how hard he worked for the company while having only a superficial interest in the rest of us. He had it backwards. Of course, we respected him—he was the vice president. But that was about all."

The effective North American manager needs to demonstrate trust in his staff and workforce in order to inspire their trust and loyalty. No doubt this is true of a good manager anywhere. But given the ongoing history of intercultural relations between the United States and Mexico at nearly all levels, that trust cannot be assumed to exist. This does not mean being buddy-buddy with everyone. It does mean something even more demanding for many North Americans—saying good-bye to personal time and "privacy" as a marker of respect. This part of trust is similar to what one would find in cultures as different as Japan, where personal loyalties count for so much. That is also what makes those of us from an Anglo tradition nervous—the dangers of abuse of loyalties, benefiting some who are undeserving while depriving others, for example, giving a friend a job instead of another, more qualified candidate. Certainly in Mexico this danger is well known. But the absence of at least some of that spirit of loyalty is unattractive.

4

The Supreme Importance of the Family

The value of individualism requires a corresponding reevaluation of the family. While the family is a cherished part of the American way of life, what is meant by "the family" and its relationship to the individual is very different from what one finds in Mexico—or, indeed, in most of the rest of the world. For North Americans family usually means parents and children, and preferably not too many of the latter. The family provides a kind of nest which the young adult is encouraged to leave some time around age twenty. This aids the independence not only of the child but of the parents. Parents should support their children to some extent, but the children are expected to make their own way.

The family in Mexico typically includes many more relatives and particularly many more brothers and sisters who remain in close contact. While differences may be great, loyalty to each other and to the family is very strong. Young people are not encouraged to leave home when they are in their early twenties. While north of the border a child's independence is often a credit to the parents, comparable independence in Mexico may be seen as indicating some rift in the family.

Such differences in the meaning of family in the two cultures influence how people use their language. Friendship in the United States, for example, is usually expressed in individualistic terms: "friends," "allies," "neighbors," and so on. Among many blacks and some Southern whites, family terms such as "brother," "sister," or "cousin" will be used to describe feelings of closeness between friends. And similarly in Mexico one may hear *jefecito* ("little boss") for father or *jefecita* for mother; the closest of friends are *hermanos* (or *hermanas*) *de alma* ("soul" brothers or sisters). North of the border the extended use of "brother" or "sister" for one not related has been part of the idiom primarily among African Americans for more than three decades. The black influence upon the speech and values of Anglo Americans has affected the speech of some feminists, too, who use "sister" freely. Thus a North American woman may feel quite comfortable in being called "hermana" by Mexicans. Anglo males, on the other hand, are less likely to be comfortable being called "hermano." However, those North American women who use the terms "sister" or "hermana" may not always act in ways that Mexicans expect of one who uses the term. This can result in confusion, disappointment, and alienation for the Mexican hermana. Normally, when people north and south of the border speak of close relationships, the North American will more likely use a word like "partner," which reflects a voluntary cooperation of individuals, while the Mexican may use a word like "brother" or "sister," reflecting a lasting bond beyond the control of any one individual.

With a Little Help from My Relatives

Questions about the family of a person one does not know well may cause North Americans some discomfort. North of the border one might hear, "I just don't know the person well enough to ask about his family." The Mexican, on the other hand, is likely to feel the exact opposite: "If I don't ask about the person's family, how will I really know him?"

The family forms a much less important part of an individual's frame of reference in the United States than is usually the case in Mexico. Neighbors, friends, or associates, even some abstract "average American," may be the basis for the comparison needed in evaluating oneself or others. "Keeping up with the Joneses" may be important in New York or Chicago, but keeping up with one's brother-in-law is more important in Mexico City. In the same way, the Mexican depends upon relatives or close friends to help "arrange things" if there is a problem or to provide a loan. While this is by no means rare in the United States, the dominant values of the culture favor an institutional response, which is seen as both efficient and fair.

Connections and Corporations

Families are extended beyond bloodlines through the institution of *compadrazco*, godfather relationships. To be a godparent is often much more than an honor; it is a means of becoming part of a vast network of relationships through which advice or loans or favors may be sought and granted. In Mexico one will hear of a person's "connections" or "influence," which is frequently through the family system.

In this regard, Mexicans show not only far more loyalty to and identification with the group (if it is a family organization) than do North Americans; they even surpass the Japanese in group loyalty.[1]

Talk of connections in Mexico is usually in terms of the person at the top of an organization, whether in business or in government. It is said that the leader of an organization in Mexico must appear to be not so different from a father in a traditional Mexican family: stern, aloof, but not completely removed. One who claims to have connections, therefore, alludes to a special and personal means of reaching a person from whom others are cut off.

The credibility of the person who speaks has been recognized for two thousand years as the factor that most influences persuasion. In Mexico, credibility is demonstrated more through position and connections than in the United States, where one's "track record" of personal achievements tends to command attention.

North Americans, too, of course, sometimes talk of connections (if only through name-dropping) as a means of obtaining special advantage outside of a system which we believe should not encourage those kinds of influences. Americans may find themselves, therefore, both impressed and somewhat bothered by such talk. In Mexico it is taken seriously because it is often through these unofficial channels that things get done.

Here, then, is another potential source of conflict between Mexicans and North Americans working in Mexico. Where there may be a choice to be made between family obligation (or using a family-related network of connections) and obeying some rule or abstract principle, Mexicans are more likely to feel pushed toward the former, Americans toward the latter.

Even large Mexican corporations (the *sociedad anonima*, or S.A.) may well be controlled by a family group, small or large, along with some close friends. It is not at all uncommon in Mexico City for one family to control a variety of enterprises. These family businesses may be completely unrelated in type of activity or financial structure. They may also be managed by high-level executives who are not even related to the family.

North Americans are sometimes puzzled by an organization's failure to take certain steps to maximize profits or to rationalize planning over a long period. Often the reasons lie with the interests and traditions of the family in control. One should be careful not to press some influential man on business matters if one suspects the man has counterpressures from the family.

And yet there are dramatic changes taking place in Mexican business as well as in the rest of the society. Changing, too, are responses to the United States. The cumulative effects of contact with the northern neighbor, which seem to accelerate and expand exponentially, give many Mexicans a familiarity with the United States and a self-confidence in dealings with North Americans that are already quite apparent. A Mexican businessman, proud of his heritage, his family position, and his education (in Mexico and quite likely in the United States or Europe, too) and proud as well of his bilingualism—his erudition, if you will—is a person to take very seriously. Many Mexicans feel superior to their North American counterparts in education, cultural sophistication, and social skills, and they prove so every day.

---

[1] Geert Hofstede, *Culture's Consequences*. (Beverly Hills: Sage Publications, 1980), 158.

5

Sex Roles and Sexuality

The past decade or so has seen an impressive effort to raise the consciousness of men and women in the United States concerning sexist attitudes as revealed in speech, advertising, and hiring practices. Increasingly in clothing and fashion, in hobbies and careers, the line between what is suitable for a man and for a woman has become blurred. If people today are not yet liberated from older attitudes and values, they are at least aware that changes are taking place. Where sexism is discriminatory in business, the issue may be fought out in a court of law.

The Separate Worlds of Men and Women

For these reasons, many North Americans find Mexican beliefs and values concerning sex roles (and the role of sex) more difficult to adjust to in the 1990s than they might have found them just a generation ago.

The American manager may be buffeted by the crosscurrents of trying to adjust to Mexican values and behavior, while still remaining true to home office policies, which in turn are likely to be supported, at least somewhat, by both personal belief and law. The manager may be sensitive to the issue of discrimination on the basis of sex, but open "sexist talk," far beyond what was objectionable at home, may have to pass without censure.

As in most traditional cultures, the behavior of men and women is clearly distinguished, and there is strong social pressure to maintain these distinctions. Women are to act like women and do the work of women, and men are to act like men. This means, among other things, that the North American male in Mexico who enjoys cooking or needlepoint should refrain from advertising those interests, while American women should take care not to appear overly aggressive in the company of a man.

Machismo

Without question the aspect of masculine sex roles that provokes the most uneasiness among North Americans, particularly among women, is machismo. "Macho" is one of those words that has crossed the border into the English vocabulary, though losing something en route. A generation ago a popular song in the States carried the refrain, "I want to be a macho man!" It is hard to imagine a Mexican singing those words, however, since one who only *wanted* to be macho wouldn't sing about it! In any case, machismo is less revealed in words than in other ways, traditionally through such means as carrying pistols or keeping mistresses. Some also attribute the popularity of the moustache in Mexico to machismo, though others believe the fashion developed as Mexicans wanted to show that they, in a race- and class-conscious society, were not *indios*. Indeed, the expression of being macho is very much identified with the nonindigenous part of the culture. Some will blame—or credit—the Arabic or Moorish influence on Spain with contributing machismo along with so much else that we know as Mexican. Machismo may also be shown through certain expressions of nationalism and religious commitment, Catholicism in Mexico being seen as more virile than either the "dry Protestantism" associated with the *yanqui* or with Judaism.

What North Americans usually find odious about Mexican machismo is the blatantly sexual looks or remarks that men direct toward women (meant also to be observed by other men) in public, in part because people are especially sensitive to "sexism" (or at least of appearing to be sexist, which is a legal as well as social consideration). There are also critics of machismo among Mexicans; Yucatecans will tell you that there is no machismo in their part of the country, further proof of their Mayan superiority. The cult of manliness, however, is not simply concerned with sex but more broadly with authority. Machismo is but one manifestation of authoritarianism, an orientation with which Americans are likely to feel even more uncomfortable.

According to Díaz-Guerrero, respect for an authority figure in Mexico is apparent when:

1. the individual seems sexually effective or when he speaks or boasts convincingly of his many successes as a seducer;

2. he affirms convincingly or demonstrates that he is not afraid of death; and

3. he distinguishes himself in the realm of the intellect, including philosophy and science.

The third feature comes as a surprise. We in the United States are likely to regard intellectual pursuits as the opposite of masculinity. In Mexico, however, as throughout Latin America, there is no such separation. Tough-minded men will proudly quote lines of poetry they wrote or reflect upon the antecedents of contemporary philosophy. Still, it is the pungent mixture of sexuality and a kind of toughness blended with varieties of patriotism and religiosity that we associate most with machismo.

The North American male in Mexico need not adopt any of the more blatant symbols of machismo, but he should be aware of styles of leadership that machismo may demand. A Mexican social scientist explains it this way: "The father in

Mexico wants his son to be macho, but not so much as he. At the national level, the President, *el Macho Máximo*, wants his people to be strong, but not so powerful as he." In relations between North Americans and Mexicans, an American manager must appear strong and competent, or his Mexican subordinates will not respect him. However, he must not act in any arrogant way so as to appear superior to Mexicans. In attempting this, anyone who assumes a "fatherly role" should be further warned that to indicate to someone in Mexico that "I am your father" may be taken as a grave insult, implying not only superiority to that person but also the violation of the person's mother.

One expatriate manager who had lived in Mexico only a few months, and who liked living there, said, "If only the machismo could be eliminated, many of Mexico's problems would disappear." A Mexican friend agreed, then added: "And much of what is Mexican would also disappear."

La Mujer Mexicana

Mexican women, at least those of the middle and upper economic classes, give considerable attention to their personal appearance. Their concern with clothing, makeup, and hairstyle strikes many North Americans as excessive. On the other hand, American women, as perceived by many Mexicans, often seem to be lacking in femininity. If too independent, from a Mexican point of view, a woman's morals may be doubted as well. A married woman who seems too independent, whether in mobility or in expressing opinions that disagree with her husband in his presence, may call into question the machismo of her husband.

The mother in Mexico holds a very special place. North Americans new to Mexico are advised to attend Mexican movies or watch soap operas on Mexican television to gain some sense of the importance of the mother. She depends upon her sons to take care of her in her old age, and it is part of the son's machismo to do so and to defend her honor at all times. Any implication of an insult to one's mother is a serious provocation. Even the Spanish word for "mother" (*madre*) in certain contexts can be provocative. Americans should take care in using the word; the alternative "mama'" is often safer.

North Americans are likely to feel that Mexican men overdo their devotion to their mothers and fail to show sufficient respect for their wives; Mexicans are likely to regard Americans in the opposite way.

There have been great changes in Mexican attitudes toward relations between the sexes and toward proper sex roles. Changes in urban areas, of course, are more pronounced than in rural Mexico or small towns. The UN International Women's Year Conference in 1975 was held in Mexico City, which some have taken as an event of symbolic importance for the host nation. Major efforts at family planning are under way to reduce the debilitating rate of population growth and, in the process, to alter some traditional attitudes, since having many children is considered proof of a man's virility and has the added result of requiring the mother to remain in her traditional domestic role.

One facet of male-female relations which has changed considerably but which still requires care on the part of one newly arrived dates to the time of the Spanish conquest and, probably, to the Moorish influence on the Spaniards before that. This is the suspicion of an almost inevitable sexual attraction between a man and a woman when they are together alone.

One means of dealing with this expectation has been to ensure that there would always be a third party, a sister or an aunt, typically, who would be present when boyfriend and girlfriend were together. Although the custom of chaperoning has declined in the large cities in recent years, it has not completely disappeared. Moreover, if a man visits the home of a housewife while her husband is away, or an unmarried couple find themselves alone through other circumstances, suspicion may be aroused in Mexico much more than in the States.

There are meanings to be read into settings and situations which must be learned if one is to avoid misunderstandings and even unpleasant experiences. A boss who invites his secretary out for a drink after work may or may not have ulterior motives in either country. However, the assumption that this is a romantic overture would be far more common in Mexico City than in New York or Los Angeles.

An American executive remarked, "When I was going to a Catholic grammar school in Baltimore, the priests always used to tell us we must not only avoid scandal, we must avoid the appearance of scandal. We used to say that what we did was nobody else's business and, anyway, we couldn't help what other people thought. Their advice, though, is pretty good here in Mexico. 'Scandal' may be too strong a word, but appearances seem a lot more important here than in the States."

6

In Mexico Differences
Make a Difference

The old distinction between an optimist and a pessimist has
it that when they both look at a partially filled glass of water,
the optimist sees it as half full, while the pessimist sees it as
half empty. In a similar way cultures vary in how they encourage people to look at a person's age, sex, role, and rank.
American culture encourages us to downplay such factors,
even though we don't always do so.

For Mexicans, such differences are very important. To an
extent greater than in the United States, factors such as age,
rank, or sex guide one's actions toward others. For example,
where North Americans may resent a person who pulls rank
or demands his or her way because of age, such behavior is
not necessarily objectionable in Mexico.

Thus in our differing attitudes about the treatment of
differences among people, we may come across some very
touchy situations. North Americans may equate attention to
such matters with prejudice and discrimination or any of the
current isms we have become so self-conscious about.

We in the United States have learned to feel uncomfortable when differences of the kinds mentioned above are given
special attention in communication. It threatens our faith in

equality. True, we may (to paraphrase George Orwell), want some people to act more equal than others—children to defer to their parents, clerks to serve customers rather than the other way round, and employees to demonstrate loyalty. And yet even in these relationships, North American ways of communicating, on the surface at least, may seem far more egalitarian than what is found in most of the world. In recent years we have learned that many old distinctions, including gender, age, and marital status easily become the basis of discriminatory behavior, and we therefore have eliminated certain personal classifications from job application forms. We've coined the word "Ms." to be coequal with "Mr." and passed laws and created company policies that express the same principle.

In Mexico, differences in age, sex, role, and other such conventions are regarded as very important. In God's eyes all people are equally regarded but a man is a man, a woman is a woman; sons and fathers are not interchangeable, nor is a patron to be regarded as merely a special sort of peon. Such talk to North Americans may sound old-fashioned at best; at worst, it sounds suspiciously prejudiced.

To a considerable extent these differences that call for attention in interpersonal communication in Mexico have their counterpart in the Mexican power structure. Mexico is a very hierarchical society, in family patterns, in secular and sacred religious orders, in politics, and in business.

This acceptance of stratification, in the opinion of many scholars, dates back to before the coming of the Spaniards. In a recent study of the degree to which people in thirty-nine societies accepted this kind of power structure, Mexico ranked second, the United States twenty-fifth. Thus, expectations as well as behavior of people relative to stratification in the United States and in Mexico are likely to be quite different.[1]

When North Americans in Mexico try to minimize certain kinds of differences in their relationships, they are likely to make two kinds of mistakes. One is to act in ways which seem to minimize differences between themselves and persons in subordinate roles, such as a maid or gardener. Americans for whom Mexico is their first assignment abroad are not likely to have had such help previously. Still, it is more our values than lack of experience that lead some newcomers to Mexico to invite a maid to dine with the family. Such expressions of egalitarian values are likely to be inconsistent with other things we do and say and are definitely inconsistent with the behavior Mexicans expect of us. Similarly, at work a manager from the States may find it difficult to understand how employees might prefer to work for a tyrannical boss who patronizes his workers rather than for one who seems to share a good deal of responsibility in decision making. The American in Mexico is advised to first come to grips with his or her own cultural values and the feelings they inspire before trying to impose these on others and run the risk of being frustrated in the end.

The second kind of mistake is probably easier to avoid. This is the failure to make sufficient fuss over persons whose age, rank, or role demand attention in Mexico. The owner of an automobile repair shop may refer to a mechanic who is older and more experienced—though who is still his employee—as *maestro*. Doctors, lawyers, and engineers each have their own titles, of course, which they take most seriously and expect others to as well. To make light of a title is to challenge the person's dignity.

---

[1] Hofstede, *Culture's Consequences*, 158.

7

The Truth and Nothing But...But...

During the world congress held in Mexico for the International Women's Year, some first-time visitors experienced the kind of problem that many North Americans have long complained about in Mexico. The visitors would be told one thing, only to discover that what they were told seemed to bear no resemblance to the facts. A delegate who would ask where a meeting was being held might be given clear directions, but upon reaching the destination would find no such meeting. "It was not that the Mexicans were unfriendly or unhelpful—just wrong!" North American managers working with Mexicans have sometimes voiced similar complaints: An employee says something is finished when in fact it has not even been begun.

Díaz-Guerrero offers this explanation. There are two kinds of "reality" which must be distinguished, objective and interpersonal. Some cultures tend to treat everything in terms of objective reality; this is characteristic of the United States. Other cultures tend to treat things in terms of interpersonal relations, and this is true of Mexico.

Viewed from the Mexican perspective, a visitor asks somebody for information which that person doesn't have. But wanting to make the visitor happy and to enjoy a few pleasant moments together, the Mexican who was asked does his or her best to say something that will please the visitor. In a land where outside forces seem to rule, these interpersonal occasions allow a person to briefly reverse the order by reporting as real what one might wish to be so. Mexicans, of course, don't have a monopoly on telling another person what that person wants to hear; it happens to some degree in almost all cultures.

North Americans have always given special importance to telling the truth. The clearest object lessons in the lives of the nation's two legendary heroes, Washington and Lincoln, concern honesty, while the presidents who have been most held in disrepute, Harding and Nixon, are held up to scorn because of their dishonesty.

Are Americans all that honest? To tell the truth, no. But we would like to believe that honesty is the best policy, and within an organization we would like to believe that yes means yes and no means no. A "yes-man" to us is one who is weak, not self-confident enough to state his own views, and even a yes-man should say no if he doesn't understand some instructions when he is asked if he does.

"As Many Kinds of Truth as There Are Kinds of Bananas"

A businessman from Vera Cruz made a remarkable analogy between truth and bananas. He said, "You Americans, when you think of a banana, you think of only one kind of fruit. But when you come to Mexico and visit a market, you see there are so many kinds. Some are big and solid and used for cooking, like potatoes. You never heard of such a thing. Others are tiny as your thumb and sweeter than candy. You never imagined such a thing. And I'll tell you, my friend, here in Mexico we have as many kinds of truth as there are kinds of bananas! You don't know what you've been missing!"

Though his analogy is strained, his point is well taken: what we expect and how we define the truth or a lie is a cultural matter. When Americans and Mexicans work together, it can become a source of intercultural confusion and conflict.

Two things must be considered. One is the range of situations in which not expressing the truth ("the whole truth, and nothing but the truth") is acceptable. The second concerns the speaker's own belief in what he or she says.

As for the range of situations, Americans draw a line between honesty and white (social) lies at about the same place where they separate business from pleasure. We may believe that "honesty is the best policy" in banking and even in government, but we don't always value candor when we thank a host or hostess for a dinner we didn't enjoy or when we meet a friend whose poor performance we just saw in an amateur theatrical production. In social settings such as these, many Americans feel much better saying something ambiguous or simply "thank you" rather than uttering false appreciation.

In Mexico, where business and pleasure are less clearly differentiated, the situation changes. At the very least, there is always something to praise, and in any case a guarded expression of thanks usually reflects poorly on the speaker rather than revealing some truth in his or her observation.

The second consideration is in the distance between what one thinks and what one says. Where straight talk is valued, the shortest distance is best. Lies of omission, for most Americans, seem less dishonest than those expressed. But where Americans may feel safe and honest with themselves by remarking ambiguously, "You don't know how much I enjoyed this evening," Mexicans would prefer to expound on their supreme enjoyment of such a magnificent occasion.

North Americans in Mexico might well change their assumptions, expectations, and perhaps their style, too, if they want to avoid feeling confused and hurt and to avoid seeming too serious and un-*simpático* in a land where *simpatía* counts far more than objectivity.

Psychologist Francisco Gonzalez Pineda has written at length about variations of the truth. Starting from premises similar to those offered by Samuel Ramos, particularly seeing the lie related to the idealization of the pelado,[1] Gonzalez sees distortions of truth as necessary to survive without complete demoralization. He says that the general recognition of this has made the lie in Mexico almost an institution. He describes variations of lies throughout the different regions in Mexico, including the capital, in which he says the use of the lie is socially acceptable in all its forms. Many of these forms are uncommon and unacceptable in the United States, such as the lie as aggression, in, for example, leveling a specious threat, or lying to indulge a fantasy, that is, boasting of an imaginary accomplishment. North Americans do use some lies defensively (making excuses), but even here the range of distortion is rather narrow. We prefer to avoid saying what we think rather than expressing an untruth. If we must say something, it is likely to be an incomplete truth. We rely on some conventional expressions which are purposefully ambiguous and impersonal ("that's interesting"), so lacking in emotional content that they offer little conflict with our feelings.

North American business executives working in Mexico complain that Mexican subordinates are prone to withhold information that is negative, even if important, and present only "good news," a problem typical in authoritarian administrations. However, misguided efforts to involve subordinate participation in making decisions run other risks. If the supervisor's actions are interpreted as showing ignorance or weakness, the Mexican worker may ignore other instructions and advice and decide his or her own course of action without informing the supervisor.

One does not need to be in Mexico long before hearing Mexicans complain of this or that deception, how disgraceful it is, and on and on. But Mexicans will also say they are sometimes surprised to find North Americans so naive or so narrow in their ways that they cannot adapt to the situation. A case in point is the kind of bargaining one does at a *tianguis*, the traditional Mexican open air market, or in certain shops. The bargaining back and forth exemplifies interpersonal values in contrast to the fixed-price system, which suits the clarity and efficiency to be found in objective values.

The practical-minded, objective customer is likely to want to get down to business as soon as possible. He or she will find it hard to maintain any apparent interest in talking about the weather or one's health or other information apparently unrelated to the business transaction.

When the bargaining begins in Mexico, the person who pays the first asking price comes across more as foolish than simply rich. By the same token, the person who refuses to bargain out of fear of being taken advantage of seems unfriendly as well as ignorant.

The Mexican marketplace is an excellent school for business and social relations in Mexico, and Americans are well advised to enjoy and learn from their experiences there. "Your southern or western horse trader," said one Mexican, "probably feels more comfortable with and is better at negotiation in Mexico than your northern business administration graduate. He not only knows how to bargain, he also knows not to take himself too seriously."

---

[1] See chapter 2 for a discussion of pelado.

8

A Manner of Speaking

A Dialogue of Plain and Fancy

Within the span of a few days in 1979, the leaders of both the United States and France paid official visits to Mexico. Some observers could not resist the opportunity to compare these men as representatives of very different cultures. A leading Mexican daily newspaper commented on the ways in which the two presidents spoke. President Carter was described as consistent with the Anglo-Saxon values of his country. He was specific, frank, and if some of the realities of which he spoke were not entirely pleasant, they were real issues to be dealt with. French President Giscard d'Estaing, true to his culture, spoke in a manner which Mexicans find more familiar and congenial. His style was more grand, his approach to issues sufficiently detached to avoid any unpleasantness. The columnist remarked that when all was said and done, and when the two heads of state returned to their countries, probably things would be very much the same as they were before they came and spoke. But, the writer added, the French president's speech was at least more congenial and made Mexicans feel better, if only for a while.

Ceremonial speaking by heads of state reveals cultural differences in style. Even more revealing are our different styles of speaking at the office and at public gatherings. From such differences in style we and the Mexicans are likely to form judgments about the speaker's personality and character.

From the North American's point of view, Mexican speech style seems excessively emotional, overly dramatic. When the speaker rises above the dull solid ground of fact in order to display a far more colorful, even flowery rhetoric, the North American may react negatively. The line between fact and fantasy, deeds achieved and deeds merely proposed, is not always so clear when Mexicans speak as when North Americans speak, at least in the opinion of many North Americans.

We in the United States like to be practical, efficient, and clear when we speak. Our line of thought should be as straight as our city streets, our verbal adornment no more than that seen on our modern buildings. While we want to be pleasant and not too blunt in what we say, we don't want to waste time with much small talk either at the beginning or at the end of conversations, and seldom in the middle. We associate too much small talk with a lack of seriousness of purpose and with "gabby," superficial people. We feel more comfortable talking about facts, plans, or matters that are technical rather than personal; so much so, in fact, that Mexicans often find Americans get too mired in details. They would prefer strong, bold outlines of general principles supported by credible personal experience. These contrasts may be observed most clearly in negotiations between Mexicans and North Americans.

We are terrified of speaking in public, and while we have a fair share of "great speeches" in our national history, "orator" today sounds anachronistic. As for a "good talker," we should be extra careful: he must be after something!

These attitudes do not always serve us well in Mexico. Our efficiency seems too hurried at times, particularly when we enter into or come to the end of a conversation. We do not always allow a chance for the personalities, as well as points of discussion, to emerge. There is thus special value in small talk and in making much of very little. If we always talk "straight," we miss the opportunity for some enjoyable excursions along the way.

A very different picture from that sketched above sometimes appears at more formal occasions in Mexico when North Americans unfamiliar with the culture are called upon to speak. Where words like "dignified" or "eloquent" might well describe the Mexican rhetoric, the North American may feel and seem to others clumsy and ill at ease. Generally, North Americans lack both the occasions and the requisite desire for speaking in the grand style. Even the word "eloquence" sounds to the ears of many North Americans pretentious, hollow, old-fashioned.

The attention given to talk of business and pleasure is different on both sides of the border. It is not as simple as saying that North Americans are all for business and Mexicans enjoy life's simple pleasures more. Rather, both the time devoted to and the timing of talk of business and pleasure are likely to be different. North Americans are likely to minimize the exchange of pleasantries and then "get down to business"; "if time allows," North Americans will return to more personal, nonbusiness-related matters. The Mexican counterpart, on the other hand, may want to spend a good deal more time in personal conversation before getting into business matters. How else can two people get to know each other and begin to intuit the trustworthiness of the other? If each were asked, the North American and the Mexican would probably say that they put "first things first." More important, they are likely to see the other as having things backward. The North American, wanting to appear serious and professional, may come across as impatient and cold. The Mexican, particularly within his Mexican setting, wants to appear gracious, friendly, and willing to get to know the North American as an individual, not a type; instead, he may be perceived by the North

American as lacking in seriousness of purpose or profession-
alism.

The Mexican Delight in Word Play

Mexicans delight in verbal play. Double entendres, turns of
phrase, dichos (quotations), expressed at the right moment
in an otherwise ordinary conversation, are an important part
of daily give-and-take. One sees a resourcefulness with language in the popular culture as well: Cantinflas is famous for
his double-talk, which almost passes for profundity; a modern
Mexican nightclub may feature as part of its entertainment a
recitation of poetry; you hear elaborate wedding speeches and
see handpainted messages on the backs of trucks; a witty
singer from Vera Cruz improvises lyrics; a "joke of the day" is
shared at the office; and much more.

Speaking, in fact, is much closer to singing in Mexico than
it is north of the border. The meaning of a song lies at least
as much in how it is expressed as in what the words say, and
allowances are made for extravagance. In the United States
we are more literal-minded, too much so from the Mexican's
point of view. This sometimes inhibits us from saying what
ought to be said in a social context in Mexico, and it bothers
us to hear things that seem to be too much fluff and not
enough substance. As seen through Mexican eyes, we therefore lack the simpatía which is so important in their culture.

At a party, men from both cultures are introduced to the
wives of other guests. The American says, "I am pleased to
meet you." The Mexican says, "I am enchanted to meet you."
That distance between being pleased and encantado is one
measure of the distance between the two cultural styles, a
distance which is but a small step for the Mexican but an
awkward leap for many Americans.

Little Words Mean a Lot

In Mexican speech, as in Mexican folk craft, diminutives abound. Much of the world is made smaller, more intimate, or more manageable through the use of those -*itos* and -*itas* and other suffixes. The word *chico*, meaning small, easily turns into *chiquito*, which is still smaller, and that is further reduced as *chiquitito*. A kiss that is sought, a coin that is begged, or a loved one addressed—each is transformed through the diminutive. No other Spanish-speaking country is so enamored of the diminutive form. The opposite form, augmentatives, is also used, but less so. In the United States, however, we tend to do the reverse. Diminutives we associate with the speech of children, but everybody uses words and phrases to magnify—it is one of our greatest and most famous habits! When we think we are being only descriptive ("Chicago has the world's tallest building and the world's busiest airport."), we may seem to be boasting. When Mexicans verbally shrink some problem, we may think they are afraid to deal with reality as it is.

Attitudes toward the Spanish Language

It would be as foolish to ignore the influence of the language difference in misunderstandings across the cultures as it would be to believe that the communication problems are due primarily to language. Mexicans and North Americans differ somewhat in their attitudes toward speaking other languages and toward the use of their own language in day-to-day communication.

Of the English language in the United States, this much should be noted: (1) Most Americans assume that everybody in the country speaks English and that most of those who do not are recent immigrants who will learn quickly; (2) Americans feel no particular identification with speakers of English in other parts of the world, indeed, not a few believe every-one in the world speaks English; (3) although there are popular books every year which complain about the sorry state of the language today and though some people are intimidated by purists and traditional grammarians, most of us feel that "the best English" is that which communicates. In our attitudes toward language, as in other attitudes, we contrast esthetics or elegance with practicality and come down firmly on the side of the practical.

Americans think that all languages must be about the same in their ability to communicate ideas, but that some carry more prestige than others. French, even English with a French accent, is prestigious. Spanish, and especially English with "a Spanish accent," is not. No foreign language is more widely taught in our schools than Spanish, and few languages present the American with as many cognates and such a consistent phonetic alphabet. As a result, there is a widely held view that Spanish is an easy language to learn, an attitude which the newcomer hears immediately. Remarks like "once you get the language under your belt" or "after you master Spanish in a few months" raise false hopes and lead to both personal discouragement and a talent for appearing to understand more than one does. No language is easy to learn for an adult, and Spanish is no exception for North Americans. With effort and the assistance of any of a number of excellent, modestly priced classes, progress in learning Spanish can be a very important part of one's Mexican experience.

Mexicans have a serious interest in their own language. In part this is due to the pleasure of verbal play and poetry, mentioned previously. It is also partly due to the more prominent place of the intellectual and man of letters in Mexico. And it has something to do with a concern for being proper, respectable, *decente*, which one hears in many casual conversations and which strikes some observers as something of a preoccupation. While facility with Spanish serves some as a mark of their distance from *los indecentes*, who may struggle with the language, it should also be noted that every year more and more interest is shown in the study of Nahuatl and other indigenous languages as part of the Mexicans' search for their past.

It should be apparent that without some competence in Spanish, a good deal of both substance and tone in interpersonal relations in Mexico will be missed. By the same token, a sincere interest in and effort to learn Spanish will help to show the speaker as more simpático than one who tries not at all.

9

"North Americans Are Corpses!"

When we say that someone is "being emotional," we usually mean that the person has temporarily abandoned reason and is making too much fuss about something. Despite our range of regional and ethnic variations regarding the expression of feelings, the mainstream American standard is that reason should always be in control of emotions and that excessive emotionality, whether filled with joy or tears, is usually un-called for (a championship sporting event being a notable exception). Thus most North Americans neither associate the display of passion with themselves nor desire to do so. Instead, for five hundred years the English-speaking world has associated emotionalism with "Latins." For these reasons North Americans are likely to be ambivalent about the emotionalism encountered in Mexico. Its attractions, its warmth and gaiety, as at a fiesta, are not to be denied; but there is also an uneasiness that reason or common sense will be temporarily lost.

For someone in the States to comment on Mexicans' being emotional usually implies disapproval, if not actual conde-scension. But that very quality of passion or emotion holds a central place in the Mexican pantheon of values. To be without passion, in sadness or joy, is to be less than complete as a human being. Little wonder then that North Americans have been called by Mexicans "corpses," devoid of feelings, without life. Mexicans perceive Anglo rationality as reaching out to deny impulse its moment. "North Americans don't know how to enjoy themselves," Mexicans will say. "They are always weighing the consequences of this against the benefits of that. You people think too much."

Giving emotion its place is an intercultural issue that raises its head in almost every situation in which North Americans and Mexicans find themselves—at work, at home, in reporting some trivial incident that occurred, at a wedding, or at a funeral. Difficulty with the language can also add to one's reluctance to express an opinion or laugh heartily at a joke, not being sure exactly what has been said. In any case, being cautious is often prudent, perhaps especially in Mexico, but among friends and associates it may come across as merely stuffy.

If one could sort out what is Spanish and what is indigenous in the contemporary Mexican character, one might say that this expression of passion is that of the Spaniard, or more precisely the Spanish male. An impassive exterior, what Octavio Paz calls the "Mexican masks," is the public face of the indigenous peoples. But even from the point of view of some other Latin Americans, Mexican expressions of emotion between people are grand (exhibited, for instance, by the great Mexican muralists). A particularly tearful and melodramatic style of soap opera elsewhere in Latin America is sometimes called "a la mexicana."

One reason that North Americans seem to lack spontaneity and passion is that we require of ourselves sound reasons for what we do and plausible excuses for what we have failed to do. Our language, comparatively speaking, abounds in words that seem to measure, quantify, and rank. We have *tons* of work to do, we *feel like a million dollars*, a party is *one of the best* we have ever attended, and here we are in a city that will soon be the *largest* city in the world (while our hometown was only *one of the biggest* cities in the U.S.A.). We seem to be calculating and comparing constantly when, in fact, we are simply using the North American idiom.

Be careful, however, about making comparisons with Mexico. North Americans do it so often about so many things, from pottery to politics, that most Mexicans are tired of hearing it. This may be especially true because so many of the comparisons favor the American side.

Remember that in Mexico they often say *"Como México no hay dos,"* literally "Like Mexico, there aren't two." Mexicans sometimes quote this with an ironic twist, but take it to heart. Nothing is quite like Mexico. That's a fact and a warning.

10

Actions Speak Louder Than Words

As important as language is in communication, perhaps even more important are all those ways in which we communicate without speaking: our gestures, our facial expressions, the glances with our eyes, how we walk, our posture, our clothing. Even the settings where people talk have a communicative function. This nonverbal communication is important for several reasons: (1) we are largely unaware of its influence, so that when there are nonverbal misunderstandings we cannot easily identify and try to correct them; (2) the nonverbal not only supports and amplifies what is said in words, it can also contradict the words with enough force to cancel the spoken message; (3) nonverbal communication most clearly conveys feelings about relationships, including feelings of trust and comfort.

Here are some things to keep in mind.

Closeness and Contact

There is much more physical contact between members of the same sex in Mexico than is common in the United States. Men greet each other with an *abrazo* (embrace), women may kiss. Hugs, pats on backs, and other physical contact are an important part of communication in Mexico.

The physical distance between people when engaged in conversation is also closer than what is usual north of the border. More frequent physical contact and greater physical proximity sometimes make a North American withdraw, often without being aware of doing so. In an effort to keep to what is considered a comfortable conversational distance, emotional or social distance may also be unintentionally communicated. The American unfamiliar with Mexican ways may likewise interpret as a matter of personality or attitude that which is cultural: the Mexican may seem "pushy," too intense, over-bearing. North American women who have comparable con-tact with Mexican women sometimes have similar reactions.

Bodies move to different rhythms on the two sides of the border. We in the States tend to use our neck and head for emphasis; Mexican movement, like Latin American move-ment generally, involves much more of the trunk. Mexican dance teachers even comment on this difference when teach-ing steps to students from the north. Our posture when seated tends to slump more, which may be interpreted as a lack of alertness or lack of interest in the people around us.

The use of the hands in self-expression is generally more extensive in Mexico than in the United States. This is the case not only in illustrating and emphasizing what a person is saying, but in the general repertoire of hand gestures as well. Not a few of those used by men are fraught with sexual innuendo. Though there are some gestures which mean one thing in the United States and something else in Mexico (our hand position to indicate the height of a person would be used in Mexico only to show the height of an animal, for example), this is not likely to be an area in which serious intercultural misunderstandings occur.

Clothing

Clothing, jewelry, hairstyle, and the like have social mean-ings everywhere, though perhaps more so in Mexico with its great ethnic diversity. Styles of dress may first communicate the person's regional or ethnic background. In hats alone, the diversity is marvelous, as a visit to a *sombrerería* will immediately show. Since status distinctions are important in Mexico, upper-class Mexicans may give considerable attention to fine clothes, expensive jewelry, and elaborate hairdos. In Mexico the undercurrent of concern to be respectable, which is revealed in conversation, is also shown in clothing. Persons from the States who will be living and working in Mexico City should realize that clothing standards are more conservative and more influenced by Europe than in the United States. Casual wear is fine for resort areas like Acapulco, but it is as out of place in a business setting in the sophisticated Mexican capital as a coat and tie is on the *playas* (beaches) of Acapulco.

Contexts

As Edward T. Hall has argued in his book *Beyond Culture*, cultures differ in the relative importance they place on words in order to convey information. Some cultures, including those of the United States, England and northern Europe, give words great importance. Those of us who have grown up in these cultures feel unsure unless feelings or ideas are put into words; our contracts are likely to be very elaborate and specific. We believe that ideas should be evaluated on their own merit—in their own words, that is—and not on the basis of who said the words, where, or when. In Hall's terms, we give relatively little attention to the context of communication and very much attention to the words.

Mexico is one culture where "context" plays a much more important role. We saw this in the discussion of kinds of "truth" and the notion of "interpersonal values." In addition, places have meaning or impose meaning, a man and woman alone in a room together, for instance. Who says something, how it is said, unspoken trust—these matters are extremely important in Mexico and should not be ignored while making an effort to understand the words that are exchanged.

11

✦

Time

If a culture is known by the words exported, as one theory has it, then Mexico may be best known as the land of mañana. Differences in the treatment of time may not be the most serious source of misunderstanding between people of the two cultures, but it is surely the most often mentioned. Several issues may be grouped under the general label of "time."

Historical Perspective

To begin with, the two societies differ in their sense of history. Most of us in the States think of our history as spanning about 350 years, with Thanksgiving and the Fourth of July being about the only national days on which we are urged to recall that past. Mexican history is far older. At the magnificent National Museum of Anthropology in Mexico City, you can walk through three thousand years of history. Mexican traditions, including the use of certain everyday utensils, go back to pre-Columbian times. Add to this the fact that education in Mexico, in contrast to American education, gives more attention to Western history and the classics, thus creating an historical perspective considerably different from what we have in the United States. The author once acquired two books, one on management, the other on Mexican psychology, both written and published in Mexico. One began its discussion with the Old Testament, the other with Classical Greece.

Past, Present, and Future

Someone said of Americans, "Always in our past the future has been present." It is true: We Americans are very much oriented to the future. We plan carefully for the future; we test the meaning of present experience for what it will mean in the future; we even greet people with "I've been looking forward to meeting you." Looking to the future goes with our notions of optimism, modernity, progress.

Some Mexicans say we are so concerned about the future that we aren't able to enjoy the present. People in the States say of Mexicans that they are so involved with the present that they fail to plan for the future. Our orientations to past, present, and future are very different, and each culture makes judgments about the other based on its own orientation.

Critics of Mexican management complain that there is a lack of long-range business planning in Mexican enterprises, with the result that some Mexican companies seek to make high profits in a short time with a minimum of effort. Profits, however, are still below what they might be with better planning and more systematic decision making, for that requires a longer-range outlook. Realizing that these differences exist can help us to alter our expectations of what might occur and our interpretations of what does happen.

It is not very helpful to criticize Mexicans for not thinking like North Americans, of course, but this is what often happens when we think we are talking about "planning" or "time." For perspective, in countries where the regard for organization is even more meticulous and future oriented, Americans are often criticized for lack of planning and for having too short a range of vision.

M-Time and P-Time

In Edward T. Hall's influential writings on time across culture, he has distinguished two kinds of time: "monochronic" (M-time) and "polychronic" (P-time). These correspond to the North American and Mexican preferred modes respectively. M-time values taking care of one thing at a time. Time is lineal, not segmented. It may not be that time is money, but M-time treats it that way, with measured precision. M-time people like neat scheduling of appointments and are easily distracted and often very distressed by interruptions.

American football is a very "M-time" game. The coach does what he wants and calls his plays. The clock is stopped by either side for strategic benefit. Players run in and out to fit the chosen play, and if there is a violation of who is eligible or not, this will be identified. From a Latin point of view it all seems impersonal, calculated, and contrary to the flow of the interaction. Compare this with what is widely known in the world as "futbol," or what in the United States is more often called soccer. This is a very P-time sport, with a continuous flow of constant action and reaction to the other, rather than the chunks of action planned one play at a time in football.

In contrast, P-time is characterized by many things happening at once, and with a much looser notion of what is "on time" or "late." Interruptions are routine, delays to be expected. Thus it is not so much that putting things off until mañana is valued, as some Mexican stereotypes would have it, but that human activities are not expected to proceed like clockwork. This writer discovered that even in Japan, a culture not known for its imprecision or indolence, U.S. businesspeople were seen by Japanese colleagues as much too time-bound, driven by schedules and deadlines which in turn thwarted an easy development of human relationships. Many Western Europeans, on the other hand, are more time conscious than Americans.

North Americans express special irritation when Mexicans seem to give them less than their undivided attention. When a young woman bank teller, awaiting her superior's approval for a check to be cashed, files her nails and talks on the phone to her boyfriend, North Americans become very upset.

It is not easy to adjust to these differences. If it helps, remind yourself that the Mexican pattern has its counterparts in cultures on five continents. The American expectations, viewed in a global perspective, are in the minority.

Adjusting the Clock

Newly arrived residents seem to learn quickly to adjust their mental clocks to *la hora Mexicana* when it comes to anticipating the arrival of Mexican guests at a party; an invitation for 8:00 P.M. may produce guests by 9:00 or 10:00 P.M. What takes more adjusting to is the notion that visitors may be going to another party first and yet another party afterwards. For many North Americans this diminishes the importance attached to their party, much as the teller's action diminishes the respect shown the customer. The corollary of this, Mexicans' irritation with the North American time sense, is in their dismay over an invitation to a party which states in advance the time when the party will be over. This or subtler indications of the time to terminate a meeting before it has even gotten under way serve as further proof that Americans are slaves to the clock and don't really know how to enjoy themselves.

For the past generation or so, time and timing in Mexico City has undergone some major changes. Increased mechanization in such forms as the modern underground Metro or the spread of television sets and transistor radios has tightened the scheduling of some events. (It used to be said that the bullfight was the only event to start on time.) The enormous growth in the population of both people and automobiles in the capital has also meant that some traditions, such as a leisurely midday break for dining and relaxing at home, have stopped. These changes are occurring in other major cities as well.

12

Special Concerns of Managers

Good management means good communication; everything already presented, therefore, should be carefully considered by a manager who will be working in Mexico. There are other considerations, however, with special importance to management. Here are half a dozen.

"The Bite"

Managers who arrive in Mexico knowing no Spanish all too soon learn the word *mordida*, literally a "bite," but alternatively rendered as "payoff," "unofficial service charge," or simply "bribe." Certainly Mexico is not the only country in which a mordida may be required in the course of doing business, and managers who have worked elsewhere in Latin America or in other parts of the world may not be too surprised when they encounter it in Mexico. However, if one is unprepared to deal with this reality or if one arrives in Mexico bound to a tight company policy that is serious about prohibiting anything that seems irregular by contemporary U.S. business ethics, the manager will face some difficult personal as well as organizational decisions.

One veteran North American businessman tells of meeting with his friends and a Catholic priest to discuss their dilemma of trying to be both good businessmen and good Christians. The priest asked them to consider the realities of Mexican wages and the cost of living before equating the mordida practice with sin. Whether or not one wishes to confront the mordida in moral or ethical terms, the representative from the States should have a clear position on this matter from the home office before arriving in Mexico.

Not Quite Complete

A beautifully lacquered box which obviously took many hours and considerable skill to create is precariously held together by the flimsiest of metal hinges. A magnificent university building of futuristic design with bold murals painted by a master soon looks tawdry; its windows go unwashed, its paint begins to peel, and cement work shows the strain of supports too weak to bear the weight. An ambitious project is planned, announced with great fanfare, then fails to materialize for lack of attention to a few relatively minor details. These examples can be multiplied many times over by U.S. managers who find in Mexico a pattern of incompleteness that is most frustrating. The North American manager is apt to assume that once something is planned and under way all will be done to complete and maintain the project. That assumption, however, is often incorrect. Relatively more attention must be given to the final stages and to upkeep than would be the case in the States.

Sense of Organization

Two multinational corporation managers, one from Mexico, the other from the United States, were discussing how they could combine their efforts to be most effective. Said one, "With your Mexican sense of personal relations on and off the job, and with our American sense of organization, how can we fail?" Replied his Mexican friend with a hearty laugh,

"But suppose we have your sense of personal relations and our Mexican sense of organization!"

Many North American managers in Mexico believe that their compatriot had the right idea—to try constantly to enhance the better features of modern North American organization without urging the impersonal, company-first kind of policy that Mexicans dislike. Although hostility toward a company policy that rides roughshod over human beings in the pursuit of profits can also be found in the United States, the Mexican case is different. For in addition to the differences in cultural values noted previously, there is also the national difference—the suspicion that the *yanqui* manager will be indifferent to individual cases simply because he is not a *latino*.

A manager from Chicago said, "A good manager likes to think he is pragmatic. In Mexico he learns that exceptions to rules—of policy or customary procedure—may be both necessary for personal reasons and downright practical. So he has to learn to be flexible enough to sometimes bend the rules to get things done. But he also has to know that making exceptions is not always necessary or practical. It's really an art, and to practice it well you have to know your people."

"Knowing your people" is an art to Mexican workers, too. Some people say that Mexicans give it too much attention. They tend to be too conscious of working for this or that person rather than doing such and such a job. This is another example of *individualismo*. In Mexican culture, however, survival has always depended more on knowing about how to deal with particular people than in fitting comfortably into a smooth-running organization.

Labor Relations

Mexican workers are protected by some of the strongest labor laws in the world, and the manager who is unaware of them will run into problems no matter how experienced and well intentioned he or she may be. Ignorance of the law is no excuse. A labor law, for example, gives workers complete job protection; after a thirty-day trial period they are regarded as virtually permanent plant employees. Dismissals require the employer to specify reasons and may entail severe penalties if improperly done. One should have a qualified attorney who can give advice on all labor relations.

Bilingualism

Good managers know how to delegate responsibility. But when their ability to speak the language of the country they are working in is limited, the matter of delegating responsibility becomes more complicated and more important. Elsewhere we have commented on language style and usage in Mexico, but here we should stress the importance of (1) knowing one's limitations in the language when it comes to hard legal and financial matters and (2) finding Mexican counterparts with whom one can work with ease and confidence. For reasons mentioned previously, people sometimes regard language as a mere tool or medium of expression and therefore assume all "native speakers" have equal skills, even though we recognize that native speakers of our own language differ in their level of language ability. Similarly, there are North American companies who place persons from Cuba, Puerto Rico, or other Latin American nations in supervisory positions in Mexico with little regard for the difficulties that will result because of cultural or historical differences. (This is not to say that only Mexican counterparts can be effective, but it does call for forethought.)

As long as the recent pattern of selection and rotation of North Americans in Mexico is continued, with stints in Mexico of only two or three years at a time, the need to rely on Mexican counterparts and to be able to work well with them will continue to be very important for most North Americans.

Of Time and Space

Americans may look at a map of the Western Hemisphere somewhat differently from the way their Mexican neighbors see it. We are likely to see the United States and Mexico as part of the same landmass, sharing time zones, and with Mexico City no further away from L.A. or Chicago than either of those cities is from the other. The rest of Latin America is mostly far to the south and, a second glance at the map reminds, far to the east as well.

Given that image, persons newly arrived in Mexico are often upset that items coming from the States, particularly machinery or materials needed for production, take a long time in getting across the border, through customs, and to their destination. Most things take longer in Mexico than we may be accustomed to in the United States, including the personal greetings, farewells and the like, which North Americans are inclined to rush through. So it is with international transport. Plan accordingly, relax accordingly, and *no te compliques la vida*—don't complicate your life with impatience.

If the United States seems close to Mexico and most of the rest of Latin America seems far away, remember there is a stronger feeling of closeness between Mexico and its Latin neighbors than between Mexico and the United States. Therefore, if there is some political problem involving the U.S. government or a large U.S. corporation elsewhere in Latin America, its ramifications may be felt in Mexico much more than we in the United States realize.

13

Conclusion

If we look to the future of U.S.-Mexican relations, what can we expect and what can we hope for? That our mutual involvement at every level and in every sector will increase, both in frequency and significance, seems certain. Whether these encounters will be generally characterized by many of the same tensions and misunderstandings that have been true in the past or whether there is reason to hope for something more positive will depend upon several factors.

Our image of ourselves and of the other will play an important part in our relations. For years Mexicans have referred to the United States as *"el colosus del norte,"* whose enormity in wealth and power was manifest in every kind of relationship. And American practices in government and business have often reinforced that image. Now, however, we may be seeing a change. Mexico's population is increasing at a rate that is notable on a world scale, while in the United States, population growth has slowed. On average, the Mexican is youthful; and Mexico is spoken of as a young nation. The average age of the North American rises each year.

Moreover, the potential of the Mexican petroleum industry has already begun to affect how Americans regard Mexico and how Mexicans see themselves. For these and other reasons, a North American member of the Border Commission

75

has referred to Mexico, not without irony, as "the colossus of the south."

Political and economic events will continue to play an important part in an assessment of our relations in the future. Matters that may seem remote to most North Americans, such as the choice of our ambassador to Mexico, immigration policies, and the role of the United States elsewhere in Latin America, do not pass unnoticed in Mexico. Any action, favorable or not, can influence feelings of trust and friendship in relations between people of the two societies. We are now seeing Hispanics within the United States playing a much greater role than ever before. The Anglo response is being watched very carefully by our neighbors to the south.

In all of these developments we will need much more information, not only about the cultures of Mexico and the United States individually, but about their intercultural encounters as well. Here we are lagging far behind what technology permits and current realities require. The very rise in the Mexican-American population within the United States may do much to provoke some of the kinds of studies that will be helpful in understanding each other across the border. This is particularly important for North Americans who, by and large, know Mexico more as tourists than as people who have studied or worked in Mexico over a period of time. At present the Mexican manager is likely to be far more informed about American ways than is his North American counterpart about Mexican ways.

One American businessman with years of experience in Mexico lamented, "The new people coming down here are making many of the same mistakes we made twenty years ago when we first came to Mexico. Why can't we learn from our experience in human relations the way we expect to in any other aspect of our operation? There's got to be a better way."

A Mexican friend sounded a more optimistic note. "Things like learning to get along together take time," he said, "and fortunately time is one resource that Mexico has always had more of than you seem to have in the United States. We have had our problems in the past and no doubt we will have some problems in the future. But maybe we will have fewer such problems if we use some of this time to really try to understand each other right now. In Mexico, my friend, now is always the very best time."

14

Some Practical Advice

Whatever your purposes in going to Mexico, you will learn more, enjoy more, and contribute more if you are continuously aware of the cultural differences described above, and if you remember to do the following:

Find Your Antidote to Culture Shock

One of the surest signs of culture shock is withdrawal into one's own world, either through avoiding contact with others or through such familiar routes of escape as excessive sleeping or use of alcohol. An excellent way to counter any such inclinations, and to come to understand Mexico better as well, is through the active pursuit of some special interest. History, art, folk craft, volunteer service, teaching English, architecture, language study...the list of possible interests that can be pursued in Mexico with gusto—and with good companionship—is almost limitless.

Explore Pop Culture

Find out who are the popular actors, singers, *toreros*, and others in Mexico today. You can sometimes do better by humming a popular Mexican tune or commenting on Mexican entertainment gossip than reciting statistics on oil output. What's more, your research will help to lead you to the "real Mexico" of jokes and slang and some of the moods of the country. Also keep an ear open for political jokes, which Mexicans are so fond of and adept at. Be diplomatic in showing that you understand, but learn to appreciate their jokes.

Do Little Things—They Mean a Lot

As with lovers, so it is with persons from different cultures. The extra gesture of thoughtfulness or concern, the willingness to take a little more time for small talk when meeting or when saying good-bye, these count. And in Mexico they count for much more than they usually do in the United States.

Keep Your Health—and Keep It to Yourself

Intestinal disorders go by many names—the Aztec Two-Step, Montezuma's Revenge, or simply the trots—but the discomfort is all the same and not very amusing at the time. Three cardinal rules: (1) take reasonable precautions at home and on the street in what you eat and drink and in their preparation, (2) don't be neurotic about rule 1—fears about getting sick probably cause more illness than the germs such fears would be based on, and (3) don't complain to your Mexican friends—as President Carter did—about your fears or your problems.

The good news is that Mexican food can be as elaborate as anything found in a French kitchen (indeed, Mexican food has been much influenced by French cooking, most obviously the bakery goods which were developed by the French) or very simple, astoundingly hot (usually just sauces) or very bland and calming. Real Mexican food bears almost no resemblance to what is sold in fast-food Mexican restaurants in the United States.

Dress Right!

Mexico City is more dressy than most large cities in the United States. Keep this in mind when planning what clothing to take to Mexico. Be realistic about the climate, too. At an altitude of a mile and a half, Mexico City has many a frosty morning in winter, and evenings can be very chilly. Give special attention to rainwear. The autumn rains can be awesome, though brief.

Good clothing can be purchased in Mexico, including both tailor-made and ready-to-wear clothes, though many people find ready-made clothes to be ill fitting. Clothes, like most other things sent to Mexico from the United States, may not always arrive as expected. (That twisted polyester tie which your dear aunt did not send was probably passed on in exchange by some customs inspector for the one she did send.) Duty for whatever arrives can be high. Plan ahead.

Say "Ah!"

When we, uh, don't know what to, uh, say, we, uh, make the most frequently used sound in the English language. The "uh" sound, as in the words "the" and "a," is the sound we make for most unaccented vowels in English. Linguists call that sound "the schwa." But as common as the "uh" is in English, it is one sound that never appears in Spanish except when spoken with a gringo accent.

Being careful to say "tor-teé-yah" instead of "tor-teeyuh" won't guarantee that you will win friends and influence people in Mexico, but it can do far more than you might imagine.

Keep Words in Context

There is considerable folklore about the origin of the word *gringo* as it refers to the *yanqui*. As informal or slang terms, they may express familiarity or contempt, or something in between. Both words should be used or responded to with some caution and with somewhat more good humor. The words "Mexico" or "Mexicano/a" pose no special problems, though "Mexico" is likely to mean the capital city rather than the country, so be aware of the context.

Remember Los Indios Are Mexicans

Visitors to Mexico are often confused about distinctions among Indians, mestizos, and Mexicans. Keep in mind that such distinctions are culturally, not biologically, based.

A person is usually classified as Indio by virtue of language, clothing, or other habits, not on the kinds of physical features North Americans are likely to look for. Even census takers distinguish Indios on the basis of such behaviors as going barefoot instead of wearing shoes or eating certain foods with the fingers instead of with a fork.

From the time of the Revolution, the Indian has been exalted in the arts, literature, and symbolically at least, in politics. Cultural divisions remain, however, between rural and urban life and between traditional and contemporary ways. In any case the people of Mexico are Mexicanos first and foremost, at least in relation to North Americans. Regional connections and loyalties, however, are often the basis for pride and identification. Family names and physical appearance will be associated with a region at least as much as with a dialect, foods, and other features, just as they are in the United States and in countries throughout the world.

Remember Mexicans Are Americans

Since there is a North America, Central America, and South America—and also, some argue, a Middle America of which Mexico is a major part—why is it that the words "America" and "American" are usually used only to refer to the United States? Some Mexicans object to that semantic monopoly, while others give it little thought. Still, you may be thought of as more diplomatic and sensitive if you refer to yourself as a "North American" ("*norteamericano/a*"). And while attempts to be more specific with a word like "United States-an" doesn't work in English, you will see its equivalent, "*Estadounidense*," in Mexican news stories. Spanish also has the convenience of doubling letters in written abbreviations for plurals: thus "EE.UU." means the U.S., and will prove handy when writing letters to the States.

About That Revolution

Perhaps because in the United States the war of independence from England is known as the Revolutionary War, some Americans unfamiliar with Mexican history confuse the Mexican Revolution with Mexico's separation from Spain, which occurred a century earlier. Such basic misunderstanding may, in social conversation, communicate more than ignorance of facts.

Mexico separated from Spain in 1810. The hero who cried "*el grito*" (independence) was a Catholic priest, Father Miguel Hidalgo. In the decades that followed, other powers tried to take advantage of the newly independent nation. In 1847, in conflicts with the United States, Mexico lost nearly half its territory—including all of those western U.S. cities and states with Spanish names. The battles of this era are remembered differently, including the cry of "Remember the Alamo," and, as mentioned earlier, the reference to the Halls of Montezuma in the Marine Hymn.

The Revolution, on the other hand, was a civil war intended to end years of oppression the Mexican people had experienced at the hands of the government, the wealthy, and the powerful church. Starting in 1910 and lasting most of that decade, it was the first real revolution in this century, with millions of people killed or fleeing the country and massive social upheaval. Since then the symbols of the Revolution have served the dominant political party, the PRI, and have been expressed in the murals of Mexico's most famous painters of the era. The Revolution has served as a backdrop for countless novels and movies—and is a source of national pride in Mexican history.

Read!

Americans in Mexico often overlook some of the most useful reading material because they limit themselves to either American publications or publications directed to the expatriate and tourist populations of Mexico.

In recent years many Mexican novels, books of essays, and poetry collections have been translated into English. Reading some of these offers the reader insights into aspects of the culture and, sometimes more important, allows the American to discuss with Mexican friends the outlook and merits of the Mexican writer.

Recommended Readings

Guillermo Bonfil Batalla, *Mexico Profundo: Reclaiming a Civilization.* (Austin, TX: University of Texas Press, 1966). For this distinguished Mexican anthropologist, the foundation of Mexican culture and worldview is to be found among the "de-Indianized" rural mestizo communities and their urban counterparts. Bonfil makes an eloquent argument for the richness and strength of indigenous culture which is often obscured by an imaginary Mexico seen by others.

Rogelio Díaz-Guerrero, *Estudios de Psicologia del Mexicano.* (Mexico, D.F.: Antigua Libreria Robredo, 1961; in translation as *Studies in the Psychology of the Mexican.*) An insightful and engaging book by the head of the Psychology Department at the National University of Mexico. Topics include the motivations of the Mexican worker and the author's original presentation of "interpersonal realities" of the Mexican.

Carlos Fuentes, *A New Time for Mexico.* (New York: Farrar, Straus and Giroux, 1996). It is difficult to choose just one book from the extensive writings of Carlos Fuentes, probably Mexico's best-known and most prolific novelist, critic, and interpreter of Mexican relations with the United States. Educated in the United

States and Mexico, Fuentes views each country in ways that are distinct from writers from either country. He has taught at Harvard, Yale, and major universities in Latin America and Europe, served as ambassador to France, written screenplays, is a frequent guest on television programs, and has been discussed extensively in magazine and newspaper columns. A *New Time for Mexico* deals with contemporary political, social, and economic events and forces as well as Mexico's attempts to come to terms with them. In this book, as in his monumental work *The Buried Mirror* (book and videotape), Fuentes excels in showing connections between the many cultural roots of Mexico's past and today's reality. Also recommended are any of his novels, nearly as popular outside Mexico as within. These include his early *La Región Mas Transpariente (Where the Air Is Free)*, *The Death of Artemio Cruz*, and *Old Gringo*.

Edward T. Hall, *Beyond Culture*. (New York: Doubleday, 1976). Through his innovative views of culture and communication, anthropologist Hall is widely credited with launching the field of intercultural communication. Of all his works, *Beyond Culture* may be the best introduction and serve both as a philosophy of intercultural understanding and a source of some very practical principles for better understanding U.S.-Mexican communication.

Patrick Oster, *The Mexicans: A Personal Portrait of a People*. (New York: Harper and Row, 1989). A journalist based in Mexico City, Oster here offers glimpses of Mexico today through a series of sketches of individual Mexicans from all walks of life—a farmer, a politician, an evangelist, a policeman, and many more. Oster's portraits help the reader appreciate the variety and complexity of people and interpersonal relationships in Mexico today, and as such help dispel the monolithic image of "the Mexican."

Robert Pastor and Jorge G. Castañeda, *Limits to Friendship: The United States and Mexico.* (New York: Alfred Knopf, 1988). These two prominent political scientists, one from the United States and the other from Mexico, present their interpretations of U.S.-Mexican relations in a series of alternating essays. Of interest in addition to the subject are the different styles, emphases, and interpretations arising from the different cultural perspectives of the authors.

Octavio Paz, *The Labyrinth of Solitude.* (New York: Grove Press, 1985). *The Labyrinth of Solitude* is regarded by many in the United States as the classic interpretation of Mexican culture. To it have been added a number of recent essays by the distinguished Mexican recipient of the Nobel Prize for Literature. The best of these essays is a stimulating piece that originally appeared in the *New Yorker*, "The United States and Mexico." Social critic, poet, essayist, former ambassador to India, Paz brings remarkable resources to his interpretations of Mexico and Mexican-U.S. relations. Viewed by many contemporary critics in Mexico as a generally conservative observer, Paz's work is nevertheless evocative and always interesting.

Alan Riding, *Distant Neighbors: A Portrait of the Mexicans.* (New York: Vintage Books/Random House, 1989). *New York Times* correspondent Riding has been praised on both sides of the border for making an important contribution to Americans who want to better understand the history, culture, and social realities of Mexico today and U.S.-Mexican relations in particular. His may be the only book on the subject which achieved the status of appearing on "best-seller" lists.

Clint Smith, *The Disappearing Border: Mexico-United States Relations in the 1990s.* (Stanford: Stanford Alumni Association, 1992). The U.S.-Mexican border is both a geopolitical reality and a fiction, a product of history and power relations, a place where news is made, and a metaphor for much in U.S.-Mexican relations. This book by a former U.S. diplomat based in Mexico is a concise analysis of historical and contemporary economic, political, and social meanings of the border between the two countries.

LaVergne, TN USA
12 August 2010
193115LV00005B/1/A

9 781877 864537